Academic Controversy

Enriching College Instruction thro...
Intellectual Conflict

by David W. Johnson, Roger T. Johnson, and Karl A. Smith

ASHE-ERIC Higher Education Report Volume 25, Number 3

Prepared by

Clearinghouse on Higher Education
The George Washington University

In cooperation with

Association for the Study
of Higher Education

Published by

Graduate School of Education and Human Development
The George Washington University

Jonathan D. Fife, Series Editor

Cite as
Johnson, David W., Roger T. Johnson, and Karl A. Smith.
1996. *Academic Controversy: Enriching College Instruction
through Intellectual Conflict.* ASHE-ERIC Higher Education
Report Volume 25, No. 3. Washington, D.C.: The George
Washington University, Graduate School of Education and
Human Development.

Library of Congress Catalog Card Number 96-76557
ISSN 0884-0040
ISBN 1-878380-75-3

Managing Editor: Lynne J. Scott
Manuscript Editor: Barbara Fishel/Editech
Cover Design by Michael David Brown, Inc., The Red Door
  Gallery, Rockport, ME

The ERIC Clearinghouse on Higher Education invites individuals to submit proposals for writing monographs for the
ASHE-ERIC Higher Education Report series. Proposals must
include:
1. A detailed manuscript proposal of not more than five
   pages.
2. A chapter-by-chapter outline.
3. A 75-word summary to be used by several review commit-
   tees for the initial screening and rating of each proposal.
4. A vita and a writing sample.

ERIC Clearinghouse on Higher Education
Graduate School of Education and Human Development
The George Washington University
One Dupont Circle, Suite 630
Washington, DC 20036-1183

> *The mission of the ERIC system is to improve American education by in-*
> *creasing and facilitating the use of educational research and information*
> *on practice in the activities of learning, teaching, educational decision*
> *making, and research, wherever and whenever these activities take place.*

This publication was prepared partially with funding from the
Office of Education Research and Improvement, U.S. Department of Education, under contract no. ED RR-93-002008. The
opinions expressed in this report do not necessarily reflect
the positions or policies of OERI or the Department.

EXECUTIVE SUMMARY

Both theoretical and practical reasons support the belief that arousing intellectual conflict is one of the most important and powerful instructional procedures available to college faculty. Yet most faculty avoid and suppress intellectual conflict, perhaps out of fear it will be divisive, or because they have never been trained in how to use instructional procedures that maximize the likelihood that intellectual conflict will be constructive, not destructive, or because the current societal and pedagogical norms discourage them from doing so. This situation needs to change, and intellectual conflict needs to become part of day-to-day student life in colleges and universities.

What Is Academic Controversy?

The path to using intellectual conflict for instructional purposes lies primarily through academic controversy. Controversy exists when one individual's ideas, information, conclusions, theories, and opinions are incompatible with those of another. To engage in controversy and seek to reach an agreement, students must research and prepare a position, present and advocate their position, refute opposing positions and rebut attacks on their own position, reverse perspectives, and create a synthesis that all group members can agree to. Structured academic controversies are most often contrasted with concurrence seeking, debate, and individualistic learning. For instance, students can inhibit discussion to avoid any disagreement and compromise quickly to reach a consensus while they discuss the issue (concurrence seeking) or appoint a judge and then debate the different positions with the expectation that the judge will determine who presents the better position (debate) or work independently with their own set of materials at their own pace (individualistic learning).

Academic controversy, structured appropriately, results in increased achievement and retention, higher-quality problem solving and decision making, more frequent creative insight, more thorough exchange of expertise, greater task involvement, more positive interpersonal relationships among students, and greater social competence, self-esteem, and ability to cope with stress and adversity. The process from which these outcomes are derived involves an opposing point of view to an initial conclusion about an issue, a state of uncertainty or disequilibrium, which motivates a search for more information and a more adequate cognitive perspective, and the derivation of a new, reconceptualized conclusion. The procedure used to implement this process consists of five steps: (1) researching and preparing the best case possible for the assigned position, (2) making a persuasive presentation as to the validity of the position, (3) engaging in an open discussion by continuing to advocate one's own position, attempting to refute the opposing position, and rebutting others' attacks, (4) reversing perspectives and presenting the opposing position as persuasively and completely as possible, and (5) creating a synthesis that is students' best reasoned judgment on the issue.

What Is the Instructor's Role in Academic Controversy?
The instructor's role in implementing structured academic controversies is an extension of the instructor's role in using cooperative learning. It consists of specifying the objectives for learning and social skills, making a number of decisions before beginning the process, explaining and orchestrating the academic task and the controversy procedure, monitoring students as they engage in the controversy and intervening when necessary to improve students' work as individuals and a team, and evaluating academic achievement by processing how well students used the controversy procedure. Academic controversies can be used in any subject area with any age student. But to implement academic controversies successfully, instructors need to teach students the interpersonal and small-group skills required to cooperate, engage in intellectual inquiry, intellectually challenge each other, see a situation from several perspectives simultaneously, and synthesize a variety of positions into a new and creative decision.

What Steps Are Involved in Academic Controversy?
In an academic controversy, students are randomly assigned to groups of four, which are then divided into two pairs. Each pair is assigned a pro or a con position on an issue being studied. In step 1 of the procedure, each pair of students researches the assigned position, organizes its findings into a conceptual framework that uses both inductive and deductive logic to persuade the audience that its position is valid and correct, and builds a persuasive and compelling case for the position's validity. In step 2, students persua-

sively present the best case possible for their assigned position, listen carefully to the opposing presentation, and try to learn the data and logic on which it is based. In step 3, students engage in an open discussion, continuing to advocate their position while trying to learn the opposing position. They critically analyze the evidence and logic of the opposing position and try to refute both. At the same time, they rebut the attacks on their evidence and logic in an effort to persuade the opponents to agree with them.

In step 4, the students reverse perspectives and present the opposing position as sincerely, completely, accurately, and persuasively as they can. In a controversy, students are asked to adopt a specific perspective (a way of viewing the world and their relationship to it) in preparing the best case for a position on an issue being studied. From preparing a rationale for the position and advocating the position to others in their group, students become embedded in the perspective. Adopting the assigned perspective is necessary to make sure that the position being represented receives a fair and complete hearing. To free students from their perspective and to increase their understanding of the opposing perspective, students reverse perspectives: Each pair presents the best case possible for the opposing position, being as sincere and enthusiastic as if the position were its own. Doing so has many benefits, including increasing students' ability to synthesize the best evidence and reasoning from both sides.

The fifth step is synthesizing, which occurs when students integrate a number of different ideas and facts into a single position. Synthesizing involves putting things together in fewer words, creative insight, and adopting a new position that subsumes the previous two. Students must drop all advocacy and see new patterns in a body of evidence. They do so by viewing the issue from a variety of perspectives and generating a number of optional ways of integrating the evidence. The dual purposes of synthesis are to arrive at the best possible position on the issue and to find a position that all group members can agree to and commit themselves to. In achieving these purposes, students should avoid the dualistic trap of choosing which position is "right" and which is "wrong," avoid the relativistic trap of stating that both positions are correct, depending on one's perspective, and think probabilistically in formulating a synthesis that everyone can agree to.

To free students from their perspective and to increase their understanding of the opposing perspective, students reverse perspectives . . .

What Is the Result of Academic Controversy?

American democracy is founded on the premise that "truth" will result from free and open discussion in which opposing points of view are advocated and vigorously argued, that truth will arise from the uninhibited clash of opposing views. To be a citizen in a democracy, individuals need to master the process of advocating one's view, challenging opposing positions, making a decision, and committing themselves to implement the decision made (regardless of whether one initially favored the alternative adopted).

Thomas Jefferson based his faith in the future on the power of constructive conflict. Although numerous theorists have advocated the use of intellectual conflict in instructional situations, some have been reluctant to do so, perhaps because of a cultural fear of conflict, a lack of knowledge of the procedures, and cultural and pedagogical norms discouraging the use of conflict. Academic controversy provides a clear procedure for faculty to use in promoting intellectual conflict. The skills required to implement this procedure are intellectual skills that all college students need to develop sooner or later. And engaging in a controversy can be fun, enjoyable, and exciting.

CONTENTS

FOREWORD

A recent ASHE-ERIC Higher Education Report by Todd Davis and Patricia Murrell, *Turning Teaching into Learning: The Role of Student Responsibility in the Collegiate Experience* (1993), reviewed the theories of students' responsibility and the research on the relationship between responsibility and students' background, college environment, and college outcomes. This research has found consistently that the more students are intellectually involved and emotionally connected with their course work, the greater their sense of responsibility for their learning. To ensure that students become involved, faculty must be willing to have students become active participants in the learning process—having students identify what the keys concepts are, understand these concepts well enough to be able to rationalize them, listen well enough to hear contrary viewpoints, and finally come to a fuller understanding of the concepts.

A number of cultural values inhibit faculty from encouraging students to enter into this active process, however:

- *Inefficient use of class time.* More often than not, faculty measure their success as a teacher by the quantity of material they cover. Rarely do they consider, let alone measure, their students' long-term retention of information. Faculty are often reluctant to use a learning process that requires students to review, discuss, and synthesize because of the time it takes away from presenting the "necessary" quantity of material.
- *Preferred position or approach.* Faculty often have developed a sense of what the preferred intellectual position or approach to an issue is and feel that their role is to tell students what these "truths" are rather than allow their students to find the truths through their own intellectual explorations.
- *Avoidance of conflict.* A primary value in higher education is the existence of harmony or lack of conflict. When harmony exists, it is assumed that everything is performing as planned; when disharmony or conflict exists, it is assumed that something is wrong.
- *Desire for political correctness.* As part of the desire to avoid conflict and the desire to demonstrate openness, faculty often avoid using a teaching method that might stimulate discourse and might be interpreted as politically incorrect or against the mainstream.

These values are but a few that most faculty hold to avoid teaching styles or techniques that might be less controllable and less predictable than lectures. But faculty are not solely responsible for this reluctance to try new ways of learning. Academic leaders, from program heads to department chairs to deans, do not value highly teaching techniques that might deviate from the norm. Because the primary form of evaluating faculty teaching is through students' evaluations, those faculty that use a teaching style that deviates from what students are used to do so at their own peril. If the normative approach is active teaching (lecturing) and passive learning (taking notes and memorizing), then teaching styles that require active learning—that require students to be intellectually engaged—often receive negative evaluations. Academic leaders need to develop multiple ways of evaluating teaching that measure long-term results as well as students' short-term satisfaction.

Academic Controversy reviews a teaching style that intellectually engages students while avoiding some of the uncontrollable possibilities of open debating. David W. Johnson, professor of educational psychology, Roger T. Johnson, professor of education, and Karl A. Smith, associate professor in the Department of Civil Engineering at the University of Minnesota, review the teaching style called "constructive controversy." Because it involves a prescribed intellectual process that takes students from researching and preparing a position to presenting and advocating their position to finally creating an understanding that all group members can agree to, this style provides for a great deal of intellectual involvement, creativity, and advocacy while also promoting the value of listening and developing consensus. The results, as the authors demonstrate, are very impressive and include increased achievement and retention, greater task involvement, and higher self-esteem.

The increased growth in our knowledge base and the rapidly changing skills needed for the future are forcing a change in the purpose of higher education. The concept that knowledge is static and finite is giving way to a realization that knowledge is rapidly changing and growing. The lecture method based on the more passive learning style of listen, absorb, and repeat is giving way to active learning styles that promote a higher level of critical thinking and a willingness to think beyond the conventional boundaries.

The intellectual skill of being able to challenge the thinking of others while developing consensus in problem solving is a skill that will be in high demand in future organizations. The use of constructive controversy is one of several teaching techniques that can greatly contribute to the development of this skill.

Jonathan D. Fife
Series Editor,
Professor of Higher Education Administration, and
Director, ERIC Clearinghouse on Higher Education

PREFACE AND ACKNOWLEDGMENTS

How students can be taught the procedures and skills they need to resolve intellectual conflicts constructively has been a relatively ignored issue in teaching. Despite the amount of time instructors and students waste in dealing with destructively managed conflicts, and despite the considerable research evidence indicating that the constructive management of conflict will increase the productivity of the classroom, instructors receive very little training in how to use conflict for instructional purposes and how to teach students the procedures and skills involved in intellectually challenging each other. In essence, instructors have been implicitly taught to avoid and suppress conflict and to fear it when it bursts forth and cannot be denied. But conflict cannot be suppressed or denied. Trying to do so makes it worse.

This monograph is about using conflict to create students' involvement in learning, intellectual curiosity, intrinsic motivation to learn, higher achievement, and higher-level reasoning. Conflict is the heart of all drama, a major tool for capturing interest and attention. If they are to learn and master the procedures and skills required for managing intellectual conflict constructively, students must do so in the classroom. The results for your students are well worth your efforts.

It has taken us nearly 30 years to build the theory, research, and practical experience required to write this monograph. In the 1960s, we began by reviewing the research, conducting our initial research studies, and training instructors in the classroom use of constructive conflict. Since then our work has proliferated. Our more recent writings on constructive conflict include *Reaching Out, Joining Together, Productive Conflict Management,* and *Teaching Students to Be Peacemakers.* Yet the concept of constructively managed conflict is much, much older than our work. Our roots reach back to Morton Deutsch and then to Kurt Lewin. We wish to acknowledge our indebtedness to the work of both of these social psychologists.

Many instructors have contributed to our understanding of how to structure academic controversies and have field tested our ideas in their classrooms with considerable success. We have been in their classrooms, and we have taught beside them. We appreciate their ideas and celebrate their successes. In addition, our thinking about and understanding of controversy has been enriched by the research of Dean Tjosvold. We have also had many talented and productive graduate students who have conducted research studies that have made significant contributions to our understanding of controversy. We feel privileged to have worked with them.

WHAT ARE CONSTRUCTIVE CONFLICTS?

The Importance of Intellectual Conflict

Thomas Jefferson, who had a deep faith in the value and productiveness of conflict, noted that a "difference of opinion leads to inquiry, and inquiry to truth." Jefferson is not alone in this view. A number of 20th century theorists have pointed out the value of conflict. Piaget (1950), for example, proposed that it is disequilibrium within a student's cognitive structure that motivates transitions from one stage of cognitive reasoning to another. He believed that conflict among peers is an essential cause of a shift from egocentrism to accommodation of other people's perspectives. Piaget proposed that a person, with an existing way of organizing his or her cognitive structures, enters into cooperative interaction with peers. Conflicts inevitably result, creating internal disequilibrium and the inability to assimilate current experiences into existing cognitive structures. The person then searches for a new equilibrium by decentering and accommodating the perspectives of others, creating the need to organize the person's cognitive structures in a new way. Kohlberg (1969) adopted Piaget's formulation as an explanation for the development of moral reasoning.

Conceptual conflict creates epistemic curiosity, which motivates the search for new information and the reconceptualization of the knowledge one already has.

Conflict theorists have noted that conflict has many positive benefits (Coser 1956; Simmel 1955). Conceptual conflict creates epistemic curiosity, which motivates the search for new information and the reconceptualization of the knowledge one already has (Berlyne 1957, 1966). Maier (1970) insisted that higher-quality problem solving depends on conflict among group members. Bruner (1961) proposed that conceptual conflict is necessary for discovery learning and can be created by presenting events that are discrepant with what the student already knows and understands, presenting "mysterious" events that seem inexplicable on the basis of the student's present knowledge, and having students argue and disagree with the instructor or with each other. Because knowledge results from social processes (that is, "truth" is derived by scholars seeking consensus through discussion), then conflict among ideas, theories, and conclusions becomes an essential part of building a conceptual structure that everyone agrees is valid (D. Johnson 1970).

The power of conflict can be clearly seen in the arts. Creating a conflict is an accepted tool for capturing an audience. All drama hinges on conflict. Playwrights and scriptwriters create a conflict whenever they want to gain and hold viewers' attention, create interest and emotional involvement, and excite and surprise viewers. A general rule for modern novels is that if a conflict is not created within the first three pages of the book, the book will not be successful.

Despite the daily demonstration of the power of conflict in dramatic productions and the recommendation that conflict be an essential aspect of learning and teaching, educators have by and large avoided and suppressed intellectual conflict in the classroom. Far from being a standard instructional procedure, creating intellectual conflict in most colleges is the exception, not the rule. Why do college faculty avoid creating intellectual conflict among and within students? The answer to that question is somewhat of a mystery.

The Avoidance of Intellectual Conflict

A number of hypotheses could explain why conflict is so avoided and suppressed in college classes (D. Johnson 1970; D. Johnson and F. Johnson 1997; D. Johnson, F. Johnson, and R. Johnson 1976; D. Johnson and R. Johnson 1979, 1989, 1992b). The first is that fear blocks faculty and students from engaging in intellectual conflicts. Destructively managed conflicts create divisiveness and hostility, so when conflicts occur among students, faculty and students may have some anxiety as to whether outcomes will be constructive or destructive. Palmer (1990, 1991), for example, believes that fear of conflict blocks good teaching and learning and recommends that faculty have the courage to promote intellectual conflict among students and between students and faculty, despite their apprehensions about doing so.

The second hypothesis is that ignorance of *how* to engage in intellectual conflict blocks faculty and students from doing so. Until recently, faculty have not had available a clear set of instructional procedures to use in a wide variety of subject areas and with students of any age. The development of structured academic controversy gives faculty a clear instructional procedure they can use to structure intellectual conflicts among students so as to result in increased learning.

Third, the lack of training programs to teach faculty how to use intellectual conflict effectively blocks faculty and students from engaging in intellectual conflicts. Most faculty members have not been trained in how to create intellectual conflicts among students and how to use the conflicts to increase students' learning. Such training programs exist at only a few institutions (the University of Minnesota among them). As a consequence, most faculty do not know how to take advantage of the few instructional procedures available.

Fourth, our culture is so opposed to conflict that faculty do not see the promotion of intellectual conflict as a possibility, and the view that conflict is potentially a positive and powerful force on learning might be culturally unacceptable. The possibility of conflict's being constructive is not viewed within the realm of possibility. The general feeling in our society that conflicts are bad and should be avoided means that many people consequently believe that a well-run classroom is one in which there are no conflicts among students.

Fifth, pedagogical norms could block faculty and students from engaging in intellectual conflicts. Current pedagogy promotes the use of a performer-spectator approach to teaching. Faculty lecture, often in an interesting and entertaining way, and students sit and watch and take notes. In an attempt to cover a whole field in a semester or a year, students are often exposed to a blizzard of information during a lecture. Departmental chairs and colleagues may equate telling with teaching. In such a climate, the norms of what is acceptable teaching practice may not include creating intellectual conflict among students.

Sixth, inertia, or the power of the status quo, may be so great that faculty simply do not try anything new. Faculty may choose to play it safe by just lecturing because it is their personal tradition and the tradition of their college and colleagues.

These six barriers are formidable obstacles to overcome if faculty are to use the power of intellectual conflict in their teaching. To give faculty the courage to change their teaching practices and to include conflict as a centerpiece of instruction, faculty members must know what academic controversy is, the outcomes it promotes, and the procedures that operationalize its use in learning.

What Is Academic Controversy?

Have you learned lessons only of
those who admired you, and were tender
with you, and stood aside for you?

*Have you not learned great lessons
from those who braced themselves
against you, and disputed the passage
with you?*

—Walt Whitman

Faculty can teach a subject by giving answers or by asking questions. Students can consider the great questions that have dominated our past and determine our present and future, or they can listen to seemingly isolated facts about people and events. If students are to consider the great questions, the questions must be presented in a way that clarifies alternative answers and opposing points of view. *Academic controversy* allows faculty to do so. Academic controversy exists when one student's ideas, information, conclusions, theories, and opinions are incompatible with those of another student, and the two seek to reach an agreement. Controversies are resolved by engaging in what Aristotle called "deliberate discourse" (that is, the discussion of the advantages and disadvantages of proposed actions) aimed at synthesizing novel solutions (or creative problem solving).

Consider, for example, students in an English class who are learning about the issue of civil disobedience. They learn that during the Civil Rights movement, individuals broke the law to gain equal rights for minorities. In numerous literary works, individuals wrestle with the issue of breaking the law to redress a social injustice. In *Huckleberry Finn,* for example, Huck wrestles with the issue of breaking the law to help Jim, the runaway slave. In the 1970s and 1980s, prominent public figures from Wall Street to the White House felt justified in breaking laws for personal or political gain.

To study the role of civil disobedience in a democracy, students are placed in a cooperative learning group of four members, and the group is then divided into two pairs. One pair is asked to make the best case possible for the constructiveness of civil disobedience in a democracy, the other for the destructiveness of civil disobedience in a democracy. In the resulting conflict, students draw from such sources as the Declaration of Independence, Henry David Thoreau's "On the Duty of Civil Disobedience," Abraham Lincoln's speech at Cooper Union, New York, and a letter from the Birmingham jail by Martin Luther King, Jr., to challenge each other's reasoning and analyses about when civil disobedience is, or is not, constructive.

The instructor guides students through several steps:

1. *Research and prepare a position.* Each pair develops the position assigned, learns relevant information about it, and plans how to present the best case possible to the other pair. Near the end of the period, pairs are encouraged to compare notes with pairs from other groups who represent the same position.

2. *Present and advocate their position.* Each pair makes a presentation to the opposing pair, with each member of the pair participating. Students are to be as persuasive and convincing as possible. Members of the opposing pair are encouraged to take notes, listen carefully to learn the information being presented, and clarify anything they do not understand.

3. *Engage in an open discussion, refuting the opposing position and rebutting attacks on their own position.* Students argue forcefully and persuasively for their position, presenting as many facts as they can to support their point of view. Group members analyze and critically evaluate the information, rationale, and inductive and deductive reasoning of the opposing pair, asking them for the facts that support their point of view. They refute the arguments of the opposing pair and rebut attacks on their position and then discuss the issue, following a set of rules to help them criticize ideas without criticizing people, differentiate the two positions, and assess the degree of evidence and logic supporting each position (table 1). They keep in mind that the issue is complex and that they need to know both sides of the argument to write a good report.

4. *Reverse perspectives.* The pairs reverse perspectives and present each other's positions. In arguing for the opposing position, students must be forceful and persuasive, adding any new information the opposing pair did not think to present. They strive to see the issue from both perspectives simultaneously.

5. *Synthesize and integrate the best evidence and reasoning into a joint position.* The four members of the group drop all advocacy, synthesizing and integrating what they know into factual and judgmental conclusions summarized into a joint position on which all sides can agree. They finalize the report (the instructor evaluates reports on the quality of the writing, the logical presentation of evidence, and

the oral presentation of the report to the class); present
their conclusions to the class (all four members of the
group are required to participate orally in the presentation); individually take the test covering both sides of the
issue (if every member of the group meets the criteria
established, they all receive bonus points); and process
how well they worked together and how they could be
even more effective next time (D. Johnson 1970; D. Johnson and F. Johnson 1997; D. Johnson, F. Johnson, and R.
Johnson 1976; D. Johnson and R. Johnson 1979, 1989).

TABLE 1

Rules for Controversy

1. I am critical of ideas, not people. I challenge and refute the ideas of the opposing pair, but I do not indicate that I personally reject them.
2. I remember that we are all in this together, sink or swim. I focus on coming to the best decision possible, not on winning.
3. I encourage everyone to participate and to master all the relevant information.
4. I listen to everyone's ideas, even if I don't agree.
5. I restate what someone has said if it is not clear.
6. I first bring out all ideas and facts supporting both sides, and then I try to put them together in a way that makes sense.
7. I try to understand both sides of the issue.
8. I change my mind when the evidence clearly indicates that I should do so.

Structured controversies are most commonly contrasted
with debate, concurrence seeking, and individualistic learning.
Debate exists when two or more individuals argue positions
that are incompatible with each another—for example, each
member of a group is assigned a position as to whether more
or less regulation is needed to control hazardous wastes—
and a judge declares a winner on the basis of which panel
presented its position best.

Concurrence seeking occurs when members of a group
inhibit discussion to avoid any disagreement or arguments,
emphasize agreement, and avoid realistic appraisal of alternative ideas and courses of action—for example, a group is
to decide whether more or less regulation is needed to manage hazardous wastes, with the stipulation that group members are not to argue but to compromise quickly whenever
opposing opinions are expressed. Concurrence seeking is

close to "groupthink" (Janis 1982), in which members of a decision-making group set aside their doubts and misgivings about whatever policy is favored by the emerging consensus so as to be able to concur with the other members. The underlying motivation of groupthink is the strong desire to preserve the harmonious atmosphere of the group on which each member has become dependent for coping with the stresses of external crises and for maintaining self-esteem.

Individualistic learning exists when individuals work alone at their own pace and with their own set of materials without interacting with each other; their goals are unrelated to and independent from any other individuals' goals. For example, each individual has to formulate recommendations about the regulation of hazardous wastes, studying the pros and cons on his or her own without discussing it with others and preparing an individual report that reflects only his or her own reasoning and conclusions.

A key to the effectiveness of conflict in promoting learning is its mixture of cooperative and competitive elements. The more cooperative elements and the fewer competitive ones, the more constructive the conflict (Deutsch 1973). Cooperative elements alone, however, do not ensure maximal productivity. Both cooperation and conflict must be present. Thus, controversy is characterized by positive goal and resource interdependence and by conflict; debate by positive resource interdependence, negative goal interdependence, and conflict; concurrence seeking by positive goal interdependence; and individualistic learning by neither interdependence nor intellectual conflict (see tables 2 and 3).

The Inevitability of Controversy

Intellectual challenge and conflict over ideas, theories, information, and conclusions will occur no matter how hard an instructor tries to suppress them. Any time students work cooperatively, controversy occurs. Any time students are asked to decide an academic issue, controversy occurs.

One of the most important sources of controversy is students' heterogeneity. America has always been a nation of many cultures, races, languages, and religions. In the last decade, over 7.8 million people from over 150 different countries and speaking dozens of different languages have come to make the United States their new home. College increasingly is the meeting ground for students from different

TABLE 2
A Comparison of Instructional Methods

Controversy	Debate	Concurrence Seeking	Individualistic Learning
Categorizing and organizing information to derive conclusions	Categorizing and organizing information to derive conclusions	Categorizing and organizing information to derive conclusions	Categorizing and organizing information to derive conclusions
Presenting, advocating, elaborating position and rationale	Presenting, advocating, elaborating position and rationale	Active presentation of position	No oral statement of position
Being challenged by opposing views	Being challenged by opposing views	Quick compromise to one view	Presence of only one view
Conceptual conflict and uncertainty about the correctness of own views	Conceptual conflict and uncertainty about the correctness of own views	High certainty about the correctness of own views	High certainty about the correctness of own views
Epistemic curiosity and perspective taking	Epistemic curiosity	No epistemic curiosity	No epistemic curiosity
Reconceptualization, synthesis, integration	Close-minded adherence to own point of view	Close-minded adherence to own point of view	Close-minded adherence to own point of view
High achievement, positive relationships, psychological health/ social competences	Moderate achievement, relationships, psychological health	Low achievement, relationships, psychological health	Low achievement, relationships, psychological health

cultural, ethnic, social class, and language backgrounds. They come to know each other, to appreciate the vitality of diversity, and to internalize a common heritage of being an American that will bind them together. While this diversity represents a source of creativity and energy that few other countries have, it also presents a series of problems concerning how conflicts are managed in the classroom. A wide variety of assumptions about conflict and methods of managing conflict can be found in almost any classroom. Students therefore need to be co-oriented as to how controversy works.

The Need for Co-orientation on How to Manage Controversy

Different students have quite different ideas about how controversies should be resolved. Many students avoid challenging their classmates intellectually. Other students believe that thinking the same as others is the best policy. Some students

TABLE 3

Social Interdependence and Conflict

	Controversy	Debate	Concurrence Seeking	Individualistic Learning
POSITIVE GOAL INTERDEPENDENCE	Yes	No	Yes	No
POSITIVE RESOURCE INTERDEPENDENCE	Yes	Yes	No	No
NEGATIVE GOAL INTERDEPENDENCE	No	Yes	No	No
CONFLICT	Yes	Yes	No	No

could confuse physical dominance and intellectual dominance. Other students use verbal attack to ensure that no one disagrees with them. Students who intellectually challenge their classmates may be ostracized. The multiple procedures for managing controversies create some chaos, especially when students are from different cultural, ethnic, social class, and language backgrounds.

For education to proceed and learning to occur, students need to be co-oriented so that everyone understands and uses the same procedures for managing controversies. All students need to operate under the same norms and adhere to the same procedures for resolving conflict. Norms are shared expectations about appropriate behavior in given situations. Resolving conflict begins with a common set of norms concerning what behaviors are appropriate and what procedures are to be used to resolve the conflict. These norms must be clearly and publicly established. Intellectual challenge, divergent thinking, and synthesis should be sought. Physical violence against oneself or another person, public humiliation and shaming, and lying and deceit should be outlawed.

What Faculty Need to Know

To use academic controversies successfully in creating intellectual conflicts, faculty must know several things:

1. What are the benefits to students of participating in an academic controversy?
2. How does academic controversy work?

3. What is the faculty member's role in using academic controversies?
4. How may students be trained to research and prepare intellectual positions?
5. How can students be trained to advocate intellectual positions through presentations and open discussions in which they attempt to refute the opposing position and rebut attacks on their position?
6. How can students be trained to reverse perspectives and see intellectual issues from both points of view?
7. How can students synthesize or integrate the opposing positions and reach consensus on intellectual issues?
8. How can faculty use controversy to make decisions?

Each of these questions is addressed in the following sections.

Your Challenge

If civilization is to survive, we must cultivate the science of human relationships—the ability of all peoples, of all kinds, to live together, in the same world at peace.
—Franklin Delano Roosevelt

History is filled with many exciting examples of constructive conflicts. The major issues of our times have been shaped by past conflicts and will be resolved through future conflicts. A democracy is conflict in continuous action. Just as it is not possible to eliminate conflict from our history, it is not possible to eliminate conflict from the college experience. It is in the classroom that students will learn how to participate in open and free discussions in ways that enrich their learning and their lives. Your challenge as instructors is to teach your students how to manage intellectual conflicts constructively and thereby give them the procedures and competencies that will allow them to live productive and successful lives.

Summary
Both theoretical and practical reasons point to intellectual conflict as one of the most important and powerful instructional procedures available to college faculty. Yet most faculty avoid and suppress intellectual conflict, perhaps out of fear it will be divisive, perhaps because they have never been trained in how to use controversy so that it is construc-

tive, not destructive, in the classroom, or perhaps because current societal and pedagogical norms discourage them from doing so. This situation needs to change, and intellectual conflict needs to become part of day-to-day student life in a college or university.

The pathway to using intellectual conflict for instructional purposes lies primarily through academic controversy. Controversy exists when one individual's ideas, information, conclusions, theories, and opinions are incompatible with those of another, and the two seek to reach an agreement. To engage in a controversy, students must research and prepare a position, present and advocate their position, refute opposing positions and rebut attacks on their own position, reverse perspectives, and create a synthesis that all group members can agree to. Structured academic controversies are most often contrasted with debate, concurrence seeking, and individualistic learning. For instance, students can appoint a judge and then debate different positions with the expectation that the judge will determine who presents the better position (debate). Or students can inhibit discussion to avoid any disagreement and compromise quickly to reach a consensus while they discuss the issue (concurrence seeking). Finally, students can work independently with their own set of materials at their own pace (individualistic learning).

Controversies are an inherent aspect of sciencing, decision making, problem solving, reasoned judgment, and critical thinking, and they are inevitable. If students get intellectually and emotionally involved in academic learning, controversies will occur no matter what instructors do. Because controversies are inevitable and cannot be avoided, educators are well advised to co-orient all students by teaching them the procedures and skills they need to intellectually challenge each other constructively.

BEST DISPOSABLE CUP: PAPER OR PLASTIC?

Tasks: Your tasks are to (1) write a group report on the issue of whether paper or plastic makes the best disposable coffee cup and (2) individually pass a test on the chemistry involved in the decision.

Disposable cups are commonly used to dispense coffee. The two most common types of disposable cups are paper and plastic. Arguments have raged for some time as to which is best. "Best" can have a variety of meanings—least costly, least waste from manufacture, fewest environmental effects from disposal, keeps coffee hottest the longest, easiest to recycle, and so forth. Apply the principles and strategies you have learned in your chemistry course to address this environmental issue. Develop a list of advantages and disadvantages for each type of cup, and summarize the trade-offs for each type of cup. The report should present both positions and provide details of the advantages and disadvantages of each type of cup.

Cooperative: Write one report for the group of four. All members have to agree. Everyone has to be able to explain the choice made and the reasons why the choice is a good one. To help you write the best report possible, your group of four has been divided into two pairs. One pair has been assigned the position that paper cups are best, the other that plastic cups are.

Procedure:

1. *Research and prepare your position.* Your group of four has been divided into two pairs. Each pair is to make a list of reasons supporting its position and plan how to present the best case for its position to the other pair.

2. *Present and advocate your position.* Forcefully and persuasively present the best case for your list to the opposing pair. Be as convincing as possible. Take notes and clarify anything you do not understand when the opposing pair presents its position.

3. *Open discussion (advocate, refute, rebut).* Argue forcefully and persuasively for your position. Critically evaluate and challenge the opposing pair's list and reasoning and defend your reasoning from attack.

4. *Reverse perspectives.* Reverse perspectives and present the best case for the opposing position. The opposing pair will do the same. Strive to see the issue from both perspectives simultaneously.

5. *Synthesize.* Drop all advocacy. Synthesize and integrate the best advice and reasoning from both sides into a joint position that all members can agree to. Then finalize the group report, present your conclusions to the class, ensure that all group members are prepared to take the test, and process how well you worked together as a group and how you could be even more effective next time.

USING ACADEMIC CONTROVERSY:
The Promise of Research

In a course on ethical decision making in a nursing school, the instructor explains that with the expanded use of technological advances in health care accompanied by the need for moral decisions, pressure is growing on nurses to be proficient in ethical decision making, and that the development of their ethical decision-making skills will be promoted through use of structured controversy as a learning strategy. "Should nutrition and/or hydration be given by artificial means to a patient for whom there is no hope of recovery and who is no longer conscious?" the instructor asks. "Your task is to write a report giving your best reasoned judgment as to when, ideally, the responsibility of medical personnel to treat a patient ends. I want one report from your group of four. Everyone must agree on the contents of the report, and everyone must be able to explain the group's final judgment to the rest of the class." The instructor then divides the groups into two-person advocacy teams and gives one team the position that medical personnel must prolong life as long as possible and the other that family members should determine whether medical care should be extended beyond hope of recovery. In addition to their textbooks, the teams have materials supporting their assigned positions. Students then engage in the steps of the controversy procedure—preparing and presenting positions, refuting the positions of others while rebutting criticisms of their own positions, taking the perspectives of the opposition, and integrating the positions.

Considerable research evidence validates the use of academic controversies. Over the past 30 years, the authors (with colleagues like Dean Tjosvold) have developed and tested a theory of controversy (D. Johnson 1970; D. Johnson and F. Johnson 1975, 1997; D. Johnson, F. Johnson, and R. Johnson 1976; D. Johnson and R. Johnson 1979, 1989, 1992a). They have conducted over 20 experimental and field-experimental studies on controversy. In all these studies, subjects were randomly assigned to conditions, the studies lasted from one to 30 hours of instructional time, all were conducted on intermediate elementary and college individuals, and all have been published in journals. In connection with this research, the authors have developed a series of curricular units on energy and environmental issues structured for academic controversies. The use of academic controversy has been field-tested in colleges and universities throughout the United States, Canada, and a number of other countries.

Several other researchers have been interested in this field of inquiry in the last 25 years, using an experimental and field-experimental format (see tables 4 and 5). Over 75 percent of the studies randomly assigned subjects to conditions. Nearly 50 percent of the studies were conducted on college and adult populations. The studies lasted from one to 60 hours, and they were all published in journals.

TABLE 4

General Characteristics of Studies on Controversy in the Classroom

Characteristic	Number	Percent
1970–1979	11	42
1980–1989	15	58
Randomly Assigned Subjects	20	77
No Random Assignment	6	23
Grades 1–3	6	23
Grades 4–6	7	27
Grades 10–12	1	4
College	11	42
Adult	1	4
Published in Journals	26	100
1 Session	11	42
2–9 Sessions	6	23
10–20 Sessions	7	27
20+ Sessions	2	8

Outcomes of Controversy

The research has documented numerous outcomes of controversy, classified into three broad categories: achievement, positive interpersonal relationships, and psychological health.

Achievement, problem solving, creativity, task involvement

While the research findings on productivity could be summarized into overall statistical analyses, the specific studies on achievement, problem solving, creativity, and task involvement can be examined separately.

TABLE 5

Meta-analysis of Controversy Studies:
Average Effect Size

Dependent Variable	Mean	sd	n
ACHIEVEMENT			
Controversy/Concurrence Seeking	0.68	0.41	15
Controversy/Debate	0.40	0.43	6
Controversy/Individualistic Learning	0.87	0.47	19
COGNITIVE REASONING			
Controversy/Concurrence Seeking	0.62	0.44	2
Controversy/Debate	1.35	0.00	1
Controversy/Individualistic Learning	0.90	0.48	15
PERSPECTIVE TAKING			
Controversy/Concurrence Seeking	0.91	0.28	9
Controversy/Debate	0.22	0.42	2
Controversy/Individualistic Learning	0.86	0.00	1
MOTIVATION			
Controversy/Concurrence Seeking	0.75	0.46	12
Controversy/Debate	0.45	0.44	5
Controversy/Individualistic Learning	0.71	0.21	4
ATTITUDES			
Controversy/Concurrence Seeking	0.58	0.29	5
Controversy/Debate	0.81	0.00	1
Controversy/Individualistic Learning	0.64	0.00	1
INTERPERSONAL ATTRACTION			
Controversy/Concurrence Seeking	0.24	0.44	8
Controversy/Debate	0.72	0.25	6
Controversy/Individualistic Learning	0.81	0.11	3
Debate/Individualistic Learning	0.46	0.13	2
SOCIAL SUPPORT			
Controversy/Concurrence Seeking	0.32	0.44	8
Controversy/Debate	0.92	0.42	6
Controversy/Individualistic Learning	1.52	0.29	3
Debate/Individualistic Learning	0.85	0.01	2
SELF-ESTEEM			
Controversy/Concurrence Seeking	0.39	0.15	4
Controversy/Debate	0.51	0.09	2
Controversy/Individualistic Learning	0.85	0.04	3
Debate/Individualistic Learning	0.45	0.17	2

Note: For a more complete analysis, see D. Johnson and R. Johnson 1995a.

Achievement and retention. Controversy has been found to result in greater mastery and retention of the material and skills being learned than concurrence seeking (effect size = 0.68), debate (effect size = 0.40), or individualistic learning (effect size = 0.87). For example, subjects exposed to a credible alternative view recall more correct information, are better able to transfer learning to new situations, and use more complex and higher-level reasoning strategies in recalling and transferring information learned (Nemeth, Mayseless, Sherman, and Brown 1990). Moreover, individuals who experience conceptual conflict resulting from controversy are better able to generalize the principles they learn to a wider variety of situations than are individuals not experiencing conceptual conflict (Inagaki and Hatano 1968, 1977). Finally, controversy tends to promote greater motivation to learn than do concurrence seeking (effect size = 0.75), debate (effect size = 0.45), and individualistic learning (effect size = 0.71).

Quality of problem solving. The purpose of controversy in a group is to arrive at the highest-quality solution or decision possible. Some evidence suggests that the occurrence of controversy in a group results in higher-quality solutions and decisions than do concurrence seeking, debate, or individualistic learning (Boulding 1964; Glidewell 1953; Hall and Williams 1966, 1970; Hoffman, Harburg, and Maier 1962; Hoffman and Maier 1961; Maier and Hoffman 1964; Maier and Solem 1952).

Twenty-seven pilots, first officers, and second officers and eight flight attendants were interviewed about how they managed specific incidents that threatened the safety of an airplane in flight (Tjosvold 1990). Respondents were asked to describe in detail a recent, significant air safety problem they had managed effectively and one they managed ineffectively. Sixty incidents were provided. Hierarchical regression analyses indicate that open discussions of conflicting views and ideas within a cooperative context are powerful antecedents to using safe procedures expeditiously.

What happens when participants present erroneous information? Can the advocacy of two conflicting but wrong solutions to a problem create a correct one? In most of the studies conducted, members of problem-solving groups advocated two conflicting but legitimate alternative solutions. In some cases, however, opposing positions can make creative contributions, even when they are wrong. The value of controversy lies not so much in the correctness of an opposing position, but in the attention and thought processes it induces. More cognitive processing may take place when individuals are exposed to more than one point of view, even if the point of view is incorrect. Subjects exposed to a credible minority view generate more solutions to a problem and more correct solutions than do subjects exposed to a consistent single view, even if the minority view is incorrect (Nemeth and Wachtler 1983).

Cognitive reasoning. Controversy tends to promote more higher-level reasoning than do concurrence seeking (effect size = 0.62), debate (effect size = 1.35), or individualistic learning (effect size = 0.90). A number of studies on cognitive reasoning have focused on the ways in which nonconserving, cognitively immature children can be influenced to gain critical insights into conservation. Presenting immature children with erroneous information that conflicts with their initial position has been found to promote some cognitive growth, although not as much growth as when they received correct information (Cook and Murray 1973; Doise, Mugny, and Perret-Clermont 1976; F. Murray 1972). Subsequent posttests taken individually after the controversy record significant gains in performance. A comparison of the impact of controversy, modeling, and nonsocial presentation of information on the performance of nonconserving, cognitively immature children on conservation tasks (the children were presented with erroneous information that conflicted with their initial position) found modest but significant gains in conservation performance (Ames and Murray 1982). Three children with scores of 0 out of 18 scored between 16 and 18 out of 18 on the post-test, and 11 children with initial scores of 0 scored between 5 and 15. The researchers concluded that conflict qua conflict is not only cognitively motivating, but also that the resolution of the conflict is likely to be in the direction of correct performance. In this limited way, two wrongs came to make a right.

Creativity. The *Tao Te Ching* says that true harmony comes into the world by blending the breath of the sun and the shade. Controversy tends to promote creative insight by influencing individuals to view problems from different perspectives and reformulate problems in ways that allow the emergence of new orientations to a solution. Controversy promotes more accurate and complete understanding of opposing perspectives than do concurrence seeking (effect size = 0.91), debate (effect size = 0.22), and individualistic learning (effect size = 0.86). Controversy also increases the number of ideas, quality of ideas, feelings of stimulation and enjoyment, and originality of expression in creative problem solving (Bahn 1964; Bolen and Torrance 1976; Dunnette, Campbell, and Jaastad 1963; Falk and D. Johnson 1977; Peters and Torrance 1972; Torrance 1970, 1971, 1973; Triandis, Bass, Ewen, and Midesele 1963). Being confronted with credible alternative views has resulted in the generation of more novel solutions (Nemeth and Wachtler 1983), varied strategies (Nemeth and Kwan 1987), and original ideas (Nemeth and Kwan 1985). Other evidence also suggests that controversy results in more creative solutions to problems and more satisfaction for individuals compared to group efforts that did not include controversy (Glidewell 1953; Hall and Williams 1966, 1970; Hoffman, Harburg, and Maier 1962; Maier and Hoffman 1964; Rogers 1970). These studies further demonstrate that controversy encourages members of the group to dig into a problem, raise issues, and settle them in ways that show the benefits of a wide range of ideas used and result in a high degree of emotional involvement in and commitment to solving the problem.

Task involvement. John Milton, in *Doctrine and Discipline,* noted that "where there is much desire to learn, there of necessity will be much arguing, much writing, many opinions; for opinion in good men is but knowledge in the making." Intellectual disagreement tends to arouse emotions and increase involvement in a task. "Task involvement" refers to the quality and quantity of the physical and psychological energy individuals invest in their efforts to achieve. Task involvement is reflected in the attitudes participants have toward the task and toward the controversy itself. Individuals who engage in controversies tend to like the task better than do individuals who engage in concurrence seeking (effect size = 0.63). Participants and observers report a high level of involvement by students in a controversy (LeCount, Evens, and Maruyama 1992). Researchers also found that individuals involved in controversy (and to a lesser extent in debate) like the procedure better than do individuals working as individuals (D. Johnson and R. Johnson 1985) and that participating in a controversy consistently promotes positive attitudes toward the experience (D. Johnson, R. Johnson, Pierson, and Lyons 1985; D. Johnson, R. Johnson, and Tiffany 1984; R. Johnson, Brooker, Stutzman, Hultman, and D. Johnson 1985; Lowry and D. Johnson 1981; Smith, D. Johnson, and R. Johnson 1981, 1984).

The effectiveness of any management or instructional strategy is directly related to the capacity of the strategy to increase task involvement. Participants' time and energy are finite resources, and success can be evaluated in terms of increasing the time and energy individuals will commit to their success.

Attitude change. In a controversy, participants reevaluate their attitudes about the issue and incorporate opponents' arguments into their own attitudes (D. Johnson, R. Johnson, and Tiffany 1984). Participating in academic controversy results in a change in attitude beyond what occurs when individuals read about the issue immediately after the controversy ends (LeCount, Maruyama, Petersen, and Basset 1991). For example, participating in a controversy has resulted in a shift of attitudes on gender issues that lasts over one week after the controversy ended (LeCount, Evens, and Maruyama 1992); moreover, the attitude change is relatively stable and not merely a response to the controversy itself.

Interpersonal attraction among participants
It is often assumed that the presence of controversy in a group will lead to difficulties in establishing good interpersonal relations and will promote negative attitudes toward fellow group members; it is also often assumed that arguing leads to rejection, divisiveness, and hostility among peers (Collins 1970). Controversy and debate include elements of disagreement, argumentation, and rebuttal that could result in individuals' disliking each other and could create difficulties in establishing good relationships. Conflicts, however, have been hypothesized to create potentially positive relationships among participants (Deutsch 1962; D. Johnson 1971b; D. Johnson and F. Johnson 1997), but in the past little evidence has been available to validate such a hypothesis.

In one study, however, controversy promoted greater liking among participants than did concurrence seeking (effect size = 0.24), debate (effect size = 0.72), or individualistic learning (effect size = 0.81). Debate tended to promote greater interpersonal attraction among participants than did individualistic learning (effect size = 0.46). The more cooperative the context, the greater the cooperative elements in the situation, and the greater the confirmation of each other's competence, the greater the resulting interpersonal attraction (D. Johnson and R. Johnson 1989).

Controversy promotes greater perceptions of social support from other students than do concurrence seeking (effect size = 0.32), debate (effect size = 0.92), and individualistic learning (effect size = 1.52). Debate within cooperative groups tends to promote greater perceptions of social support than does individualistic learning (effect size = 0.85). These findings corroborate previous findings that cooperative experiences promote greater perceptions of peer task support than do competitive or individualistic learning situations (D. Johnson and R. Johnson 1983).

The combination of a frank exchange of ideas and a positive climate of friendship and support not only leads to more productive decision making and greater learning, but also disconfirms the myth that conflict leads to divisiveness and dislike.

Psychological health and social competence

The aspect of psychological health that has been most frequently examined in the research on controversy is self-esteem. Controversy promotes higher self-esteem than do concurrence seeking (effect size = 0.39), debate (effect size = 0.51), and individualistic learning (effect size = 0.85). Debate promotes higher self-esteem than does individualistic learning (effect size = 0.45). A series of studies on resilience in the face of adversity found problem-solving skills and qualities like empathy to be directly related to students and their long-term coping with adversity (Ann Mastern and Norman Garmezy at the University of Minnesota). Mastern says that both problem-solving skills and empathy can be improved through training in conflict management. Competent students tend to be more cooperative (as opposed to disruptive) and more proactive and involved (as opposed to withdrawn). The more students learn how to take a cooper-

> **Debate tended to promote greater interpersonal attraction among participants than did individualistic learning**

ative approach to managing conflicts through joint problem solving, the healthier psychologically they tend to be and the better able they are to deal with stress and adversity. Students who cannot cope with the challenges they face tend not to know what to do when faced with conflicts and misfortune. A student carries skills in dealing with controversy wherever he or she goes, and, once acquired, those skills cannot be taken away. Knowing procedures and having skills to derive creative syntheses that solve joint problems prepares students to handle conflict and cope with life's challenges and unforeseen adversities.

Summary

Academic controversy, structured appropriately, results in increased achievement and retention, higher-quality problem solving and decision making, more frequent creative insight, more thorough exchange of expertise, and greater task involvement; more positive interpersonal relationships among students; and greater social competence, self-esteem, and ability to cope with stress and adversity. The next task is to learn by what process those outcomes are derived.

LIGHT: PARTICLE OR WAVE?

Tasks: Your tasks are to (1) write a group report on the issue of whether light is a particle or a wave and (2) individually past a test on the information involved in the decision.

Physicists have long argued about the nature of light—about whether it is a particle or a wave. Sir Isaac Newton, English mathematician and physicist, described light as an emission of particles, while Dutch astronomer, mathematician, and physicist Christiaan Huygens developed the theory that light travels by a wave motion. Light actually exhibits qualities of both particles and waves. Your task is to review the arguments supporting both of these positions, clarify the support for each, and deepen your understanding of the nature of light. Apply the principles and strategies you have learned to address this issue. The report should present both positions and provide details of the advantages and disadvantages of each theory of light.

Cooperative: Write one report for the group of four. All members have to agree. Everyone has to be able to explain the choice made and the reasons the choice is a good one. To help you write the best report possible, your group of four has been divided into two pairs. One pair has been assigned the position that light is a particle, the other that light is a wave.

Procedure:

1. *Research and prepare your position.* Your group of four has been divided into two pairs. Each pair is to make a list of reasons supporting its position and plan how to present the best case for its position to the other pair.

2. *Present and advocate your position.* Forcefully and persuasively present the best case for your list to the opposing pair. Be as convincing as possible. Take notes and clarify anything you do not understand when the opposing pair presents its position.

3. *Open discussion (advocate, refute, rebut).* Argue forcefully and persuasively for your position. Critically evaluate and challenge the opposing pair's list and reasoning and defend your reasoning from attack.

4. *Reverse perspectives.* Reverse perspectives and present the best case for the opposing position. The opposing pair will do the same. Strive to see the issue from both perspectives simultaneously.

5. *Synthesize.* Drop all advocacy. Synthesize and integrate the best advice and reasoning from both sides into a joint position that all members can agree to. Then finalize the group report, present your conclusions to the class, ensure that all group members are prepared to take the test, and process how well you worked together as a group and how you could be even more effective next time.

HOW CONTROVERSY WORKS

Rique Campa, a professor in the Department of Fisheries and Wildlife at Michigan State University, asks his classes whether a marina can be developed in an environmentally sensitive area where piping plovers (shorebirds) have a breeding ground. He assigns students to groups of four, divides each group into two pairs, and assigns one pair the developer's position and the other the Department of Natural Resources's position. Following the structured procedure for academic controversy over several class periods, he requires students to research the issue extensively, prepare a persuasive case for their position, present their position in a compelling and interesting way, refute the opposing position while rebutting criticisms of their position, take the opposing perspectives, and synthesize the positions. Thus, the professor puts into practice the theoretical process of controversy.

The Process of Controversy, Debate, And Concurrence Seeking

> *Since the general or prevailing opinion on any subject is rarely or never the whole truth, it is only by the collision of adverse opinion that the remainder of the truth has any chance of being supplied.*
>
> —John Stuart Mill

Given that controversy tends to promote higher productivity, more positive relationships, and higher self-esteem than concurrence seeking, debate, or individualistic learning, one must ask how it does so and what the underlying processes are. A number of psychologists in several fields—developmental (Hunt 1964; Kohlberg 1969; Piaget 1948, 1950); cognitive (Berlyne 1966; Hammond 1965); social (Janis 1982; D. Johnson 1970, 1979, 1980; D. Johnson and F. Johnson 1997; D. Johnson, F. Johnson, and R. Johnson 1976; D. Johnson and R. Johnson 1979, 1989, 1992a; D. Johnson, R. Johnson, and Smith 1989; Maier 1970); and organizational (Maier 1970)—have theorized about the processes through which conflict leads to higher productivity, more positive relationships, and higher self-esteem. On the basis of these scholars' work, we propose the following process (see figure 1):

1. When individuals are presented with a problem to solve or decision to make, they reach an initial conclusion

based on categorizing and organizing incomplete information, their limited experiences, and their specific perspective.

2. When individuals present their conclusion and its rationale to others, they engage in cognitive rehearsal, deepen their understanding of their position, and discover higher-level reasoning strategies.

3. When individuals are confronted by other people with different conclusions based on other people's information, experiences, and perspectives, they become uncertain as to the correctness of their views. A state of conceptual conflict or disequilibrium is aroused.

4. Uncertainty, conceptual conflict, or disequilibrium motivates an active search for more information, new experiences, and a more adequate cognitive perspective and reasoning process (i.e., epistemic curiosity) in hopes of resolving the uncertainty. The search stimulates divergent attention and thought.

5. By adapting their cognitive perspective and reasoning through understanding and accommodating the perspective and reasoning of others, individuals derive a new, reconceptualized, and reorganized conclusion. They detect novel solutions and decisions that, on balance, are qualitatively better.

Step 1: Organizing information and deriving conclusions

The process of controversy begins with students being asked to consider a problem, issue, or question. To do so, they must conceptualize, and they must avoid barriers to conceptualizing. To do so involves forming concepts, interrelating them into a conceptual structure, and logically deriving conclusions. Among other things, conceptualizing promotes learning, retention, and the transfer and application of learning.

Anything that interferes with the process of conceptualizing is a barrier to problem solving, decision making, and learning. Three interrelated barriers could interfere: uncritically giving one's dominant response to the situation, mental sets, and fixation on the first satisfactory solution generated. First, when responses are arranged hierarchically (Berlyne 1965; Maier 1970), individuals confronted with a problem may quickly respond with their dominant response (without thinking of, evaluating, and choosing among the proper alternatives). Dominant responses based on physical states like hunger can affect which stimuli a person attends to (Levine, Chein, and Murphy 1942; McClelland and Atkinson 1948), psychological states, such as attitudes and beliefs (Allport and Postman 1945; Iverson and Schwab 1967), and one's general cultural frame of reference (Bartlett 1932). Second, mental sets can cause the same words to have different meanings for different persons (Foley and MacMillan 1943), the adoption of solutions that have been previously useful (Luchins 1942), the perception only of what is expected (Neisser 1954), and the interpretation of ambiguous events in ways that confirm expectations (Bruner and Minturn 1955). Third, individuals may become fixated on the first reasonable solution thought of (Simon 1976)—called *satisficing*.

FIGURE 1

The Process of Controversy

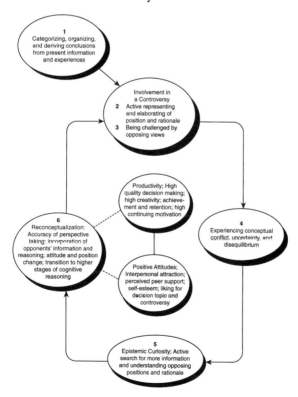

Source: D. Johnson and R. Johnson 1987.

These barriers reflect the fact that in many instances people are lazy cognitive processors (they do not actively process the information that is available or do not fully consider the alternative ways of understanding such information [Langer, Blank, and Chanowitz 1978; Taylor 1980]) and do not think divergently. Divergent thinking results in more ideas (fluency) and more classes of ideas (flexibility) (Guilford 1956). To ensure that divergent thinking takes place and all major alternatives to the problem being considered are given a fair hearing, each alternative has to be presented completely and persuasively.

Organizing information to derive a conclusion, with the knowledge that it will be presented to other people, results in individuals' understanding the information better than if they were organizing it for their own use (Allen 1976; Benware 1975; Gartner, Kohler, and Reissman 1971). Higher-level conceptual understanding and reasoning are promoted when individuals know they have to teach each other a common way to think about problem situations (D. Johnson and R. Johnson 1979, 1983; F. Murray 1983). The way people conceptualize and organize material cognitively has been found to be markedly different when they learned material to teach to others and when they learned material for their own benefit (Annis 1983; Bargh and Schul 1980; F. Murray 1983).

Under certain conditions, individuals will gather and organize facts, information, and theories into a rationale; under other conditions, they will not. The adequacy of a person's preparation depends largely on the skills of searching out relevant evidence and organizing it into a coherent and logical rationale (D. Johnson and F. Johnson 1997); the effort expended, as individuals generally have an enhanced regard for their own productions relative to others' (Greenwald and Albert 1968) and the effort spent in preparing a position may be a source of enhanced regard for one's own position (Zimbardo 1965); and the degree to which individuals are task oriented, not ego oriented (ego-oriented efforts tend to focus on proving one is "right" and "better," while task-oriented efforts tend to focus on contributing to a process of making the best decision possible) (Nicholls 1983).

Step 2: Presenting and advocating conclusions and rationale

Advocacy is presenting a conclusion and providing reasons why others should adopt it. Individuals engaged in controversy (compared with those engaged in debate, concurrence seeking, and individualistic learning) contribute more information to the discussion, more frequently repeat information, share new information, elaborate the material being discussed, present more ideas, present more rationale, make more higher-level processing statements, make more comments aimed at managing their efforts to make high-quality decisions, make fewer intermediate-level cognitive processing statements, and make more statements managing the group's work (D. Johnson and R. Johnson 1985; D. Johnson et al. 1985; D. Johnson, R. Johnson, and Tiffany 1984; Lowry and D. Johnson 1981; Nijhof and Kommers 1982; Smith, D. Johnson, and R. Johnson 1981, 1984). Disagreements within a group provide more information and a greater variety of facts as well as more changes in the salience of known information (Anderson and Graesser 1976; Kaplan 1977; Kaplan and Miller 1977; Vinokur and Burnstein 1974). Peers, moreover, have frequently been found to be more effective in teaching information to their peers than specially trained experts (Fisher 1969; Sarbin 1976). Finally, people are particularly prone to increase their commitment to a cause that they attempted to persuade another to adopt (Nel, Helmreich, and Aronson 1969).

For the presentation to be credible and to have an impact on the other participants in a controversy, a position must be persistently presented with consistency and confidence and, if possible, advocated by more than one person (Nemeth, Swedlund, and Kanki 1974; Nemeth and Wachtler 1983).

Step 3: Uncertainty created by being challenged by opposing views

Students tend to experience conceptual conflict and uncertainty when faced with opposing positions and challenges to the validity of their own position. The direct evidence indicates that the greater the disagreement among group members, the more frequently disagreement occurs, the greater the number of people disagreeing with a person's position, the more competitive the context of the controversy, and the more affronted the person feels, the greater the conceptual conflict and uncertainty the person experiences (Asch 1952; Burdick and Burnes 1958; Festinger and Maccoby 1964; Gerard and Greenbaum 1962; Inagaki and Hatano 1968, 1977; Lowry and D. Johnson 1981; Tjosvold and D. Johnson 1977, 1978; Tjosvold, D. Johnson, and Fabrey 1980; Worchel and McCormick 1963).

For cognitive conflict and uncertainty to be maximized, students must be free to express their opinions, accurately perceive opposing information and reasoning, not be overloaded with information, see opposing information as useful, be challenged by a majority of group members, and be challenged by valid information.

Having the freedom to express independent opinions. Exposure to more than one point of view decreases the tendency to conform to the majority opinion and to accept uncritically the opinions of others (Asch 1956). Hearing opposing views gives participants the freedom to examine alternative and original solutions to problems without the stress of noncompliance to the majority opinion (Nemeth 1986).

Misperceiving opposing information and reasoning. Seeking to understand the rationale supporting opposing positions is not a simple enterprise, and understanding information contradicting one's own position and reasoning is subject to bias and selective perception in a number of ways. First, individuals tend to seek, learn, and recall information that confirms and supports their beliefs (Levine and Murphy 1943; Nisbett and Ross 1980; Snyder and Cantor 1979; Swann and Reid 1981). For example, individuals learn and retain information congruent with their positions better than they do statements that run counter to their positions (Levine and Murphy 1943). Second, individuals with certain expectations will perceive some information and events but not others (Dearborn and Simon 1958; Foley and MacMillan 1943; Iverson and Schwab 1967; Neisser 1954; Postman and Brown 1952). Third, individuals' preconceptions and perspectives affect their understanding and recall of information (Allport and Postman 1945; Bartlett 1932; Pepitone 1950). Finally, individuals who hold strong beliefs about an issue are apt to subject disconfirming evidence to highly critical evaluation while accepting confirming evidence at face value (Lord, Ross, and Lepper 1979).

Being overloaded with opposing information. Some danger of information overload and becoming confused with the complexity of the issues exists when we are required to learn opposing views and contrary information. The amount of information human beings can process at any given time is limited. If they are exposed to more information than they can handle, much of it will be lost. Sometimes, in the interests of accuracy or objectivity, so much information is packed into such a short period of time that nearly everything is lost—called "information overload."

Perceiving the usefulness of the opposing position. If individuals plan to use contrary information to improve the quality of their learning, problem solving, or decision making, they tend to learn and use the information. For example, when individuals have to learn information counter to their position because they have to be ready to argue from that viewpoint later, they learn it better than those who agree with the information and therefore already have such arguments at hand (Jones and Aneshansel 1956).

Being challenged by a majority or minority. Whether individuals' views are challenged by a majority or a minority of group members has important implications for the outcomes of controversy. Majorities exert more influence than do minorities (see Tanford and Penrod 1984 for a review). Majorities may influence through compliance (through the process of comparison) or conversion (through the process of validation). In most groups, movement is toward the majority opinion. A study of 225 juries, for example, documented that the majority position on the first ballot (that is, the position held by seven to 11 jury members) was the final verdict in over 85 percent of the cases (Kalven and Zeisel 1966). Such movement to the majority position is assumed to be based on information influence (majority judgments give information about reality) and normative influence (individuals want to be accepted and avoid disapproval) (Deutsch and Gerard 1955). Majorities start with positive judgments and expectations (that is, they are correct and their approval is important). Movement to the majority position usually occurs early during a group discussion (Asch 1956). Majority viewpoints seem to be seriously considered from the beginning, and majority influence often results in overt compliance without private or latent change to majority views (Allen 1965; Moscovici and Lage 1976). Two types of conflict are aroused by the majority: the fear of being deviant and the fear of being wrong.

Majorities induce a concentration on the position they propose (Nemeth 1976, 1986). Persons exposed to opposing majority views focus on the aspects of the stimuli pertinent to the position of the majority, they think in convergent ways, and they tend toward adoption of the proposed solution to the neglect of novel solutions or decisions. The quality of the solution or decision depends on the validity of the initial majority position.

Being influenced by a minority is different. Minorities have to convert through validating their position. The conflict aroused is based on the fear of being wrong (resistance to agreeing with a minority position, however, may be aroused by not wanting to lose membership in the majority). Minorities are often viewed negatively, sometimes with downright derision (Nemeth and Wachtler 1983). Movement to the minority position often occurs late in the group discussion (Nemeth, Swedlund, and Kanki 1974; Nemeth and Wachtler 1974, 1983). Minority viewpoints need time to be accepted because it is the consistency and confidence with which the minority positions are argued that leads them to receive serious consideration (Moscovici and Faucheaux 1972; Moscovici and Nemeth 1974). Minority influences may be latent, being detected in subsequent situations where individuals make solitary judgments (Moscovici and Lage 1976; Moscovici, Lage, and Naffrechoux 1969; Mugny 1980; Nemeth and Wachtler 1974).

Minorities, compared with majorities, stimulate a greater consideration of other alternatives, and persons exposed to opposing minority views therefore exert more cognitive effort (Nemeth 1976, 1986). Those exposed to minority views are stimulated to attend to more aspects of the situation, they think in more divergent ways, and they are more likely to detect novel solutions or come to new decisions. On balance, these solutions and decisions are "better" or "more correct." Initially, opposing minority views are considered to be incorrect and are dismissed. But with the minority's consistency and confidence over time, individuals may ask, "How can they be so wrong and yet so sure of themselves?" As a result, they are stimulated to reappraise the entire situation, which may include alternatives other than the one being proposed by the minority. In other words, the thought processes are marked by divergence, and the potential for detecting novel solutions or decisions is therefore present.

Much more stress is reported in situations involving majority influence than in those involving minority influence, presumably because in the former individuals feared they were wrong and the majority would reject them while in the latter individuals could deride the minority and their opposing views (Asch 1956; Maass and Clark 1984; Nemeth 1976; Nemeth and Wachtler 1983). The stress induced by the majority would be expected to narrow the focus of attention and increase the likelihood that the strongest and most dominant response would be engaged in (Zajonc 1965). The more moderate stress experienced when facing minority opposition may stimulate individuals to consider more aspects of the situation and more possible conclusions.

Being challenged by a valid or erroneous position.
Participants exposed to a credible but erroneous minority view generate more solutions to a problem and more correct solutions than do subjects exposed to a consistent single view and engaged in more cognitive processing (Nemeth and Wachtler 1983). The advance to higher-level reasoning results from being confronted with an opposing erroneous point of view (Cook and Murray 1973; Doise, Mugny, and Perret-Clermont 1976; J. Murray 1974).

Summary. The direct evidence indicates that opposing information is learned more accurately during controversies than during debate, concurrence seeking, or individualistic learning. Hearing opposing views being advocated furthermore stimulates new cognitive analysis and frees individuals to create alternative and original conclusions. When contrary information is not clearly relevant to completing the task at hand, it may be ignored, discounted, or perceived in biased ways in favor of supporting evidence. When individuals realize, however, that they are accountable for knowing the contrary information some time in the near future, they tend to learn it. Too much information can result in information overload. Opposing views are more effective in promoting divergent thinking and effective problem solving when they are presented by a minority. Even being confronted with an erroneous point of view can result in more divergent thinking and the generation of novel and more cognitively advanced solutions.

Hearing opposing views being advocated furthermore stimulates new cognitive analysis and frees individuals to create alternative and original conclusions.

Step 4: Epistemic curiosity and perspective taking
When faced with intellectual opposition within a cooperative context, individuals tend to experience uncertainty, disequilibrium, or conceptual conflict. Conceptual conflict is

hypothesized to motivate an active search for more information (often called epistemic curiosity) in hopes of resolving the uncertainty. The direct evidence indicates that individuals engaged in controversy (compared to persons involved in noncontroversial discussions, concurrence-seeking discussions, and individualistic learning) are motivated to know others' positions and to develop an understanding and appreciation of them (Tjosvold and D. Johnson 1977, 1978; Tjosvold, D. Johnson, and Fabrey 1980; Tjosvold, D. Johnson, and Lerner 1981) and in fact do develop a more accurate understanding of other positions (Smith, D. Johnson, and R. Johnson 1981; Tjosvold and D. Johnson 1977, 1978; Tjosvold, D. Johnson, and Fabrey 1980). Indices of epistemic curiosity include individuals' actively searching for more information, seeking to understand opposing positions and rationales, and attempting to view the situation from opposing perspectives.

Searching for information. Some evidence suggests that controversy results in an active search for more information. For example, individuals involved in controversy, compared with persons involved in concurrence seeking, read more relevant material, review more relevant materials, more frequently gather further information during their free time, and more frequently request information from others (Lowry and D. Johnson 1981). Controversy, compared with both concurrence seeking and individualistic learning, promotes greater use of relevant materials and more frequently giving up free time to gather further information (Smith, D. Johnson, and R. Johnson 1981). Controversy, compared with debate and individualistic learning, promotes greater searches for more information outside of class (D. Johnson and R. Johnson 1985; D. Johnson, R. Johnson, and Tiffany 1984). Individuals engaged in controversy have greater interest in learning more about the subject being discussed than do persons engaged in concurrence seeking or individualistic learning (R. Johnson et al. 1985). Small discussion groups working cooperatively consulted more books in writing papers for a college psychology course than did individuals in a traditional lecture-competition format (Beach 1974). Individuals participating in cooperative discussion groups during a college psychology course engaged in more serious reading to increase their knowledge and demonstrated more curiosity about the subject matter following a course than did individuals in a traditional lecture-competition course format (Hovey, Gruber, and Terrell 1963).

Seeking to understand opposing positions. Individuals engaged in controversy seek to know, understand, and appreciate opposing positions (Tjosvold and D. Johnson 1977, 1978; Tjosvold, D. Johnson, and Fabrey 1980; Tjosvold, D. Johnson, and Lerner 1981). Attempting to understand opposing positions pays off. Individuals involved in a controversy develop a more accurate understanding of other positions than do persons involved in noncontroversial discussions, concurrence-seeking discussions, and individualistic learning (Smith, D. Johnson, and R. Johnson 1981; Tjosvold and D. Johnson 1977, 1978; Tjosvold, D. Johnson, and Fabrey 1980).

Viewing the situation from different perspectives. To arrive at a synthesis that is acceptable to all group members, the issue must be viewed from all perspectives. Group members need to be able to both comprehend the information being presented by their opposition and understand the cognitive perspective being used to organize and interpret that information. A cognitive perspective consists of the cognitive organization being used to give meaning to a person's knowledge and the structure of a person's reasoning. The presence of controversy promotes greater understanding of another person's cognitive perspective than does the absence of controversy (Tjosvold and D. Johnson 1977, 1978; Tjosvold, D. Johnson, and Fabrey 1980). Individuals engaging in a controversy are better able subsequently to predict what line of reasoning their opponent will use in solving a future problem than are persons who interact without any controversy. For example, individuals engaged in a controversy are more accurate in understanding their opponents' perspective than are those involved in concurrence-seeking discussions or individualistic learning (Smith, D. Johnson, and R. Johnson 1981). Moreover, individuals engaged in controversy are better able to take the opposing perspective than are individuals participating in concurrence-seeking discussions (D. Johnson et al. 1985). Finally, perspective-taking skills are important for exchanging information and opinions within a controversy, affecting the amount of information disclosed, communication skills, accuracy of understanding and retention of opposing positions, and friendliness of the information exchange (D. Johnson 1971a).

Step 5: Reconceptualization, synthesis, and integration
When overt controversy is structured within a problem-solving, decision-making, or learning group by identifying alternatives and assigning members to advocate the best case for each alternative, the purpose is not to choose the best alternative but to create a synthesis of the best reasoning and conclusions from all the various alternatives. Synthesizing occurs when individuals integrate a number of different ideas and facts into a single position. It may be hypothesized that the quality of individuals' reconceptualization, synthesis, and integration depends on the accuracy of their perspective taking, their incorporation of others' information and reasoning into their own position, their change in attitude and position, and their transition to higher stages of cognitive reasoning.

Incorporating others' information and reasoning. Participation in a controversy, compared with participation in noncontroversial discussions, concurrence-seeking discussions, and individualistic learning, results in greater incorporation of opponents' arguments and information (D. Johnson and R. Johnson 1985; D. Johnson, R. Johnson, and Tiffany 1984; Tjosvold, D. Johnson, and Lerner 1981). Two conditions hypothetically affect the incorporation of opposing information: whether cooperative or competitive elements dominate the situation, and whether participants disagree skillfully or unskillfully. When the context is cooperative, participants listen more open-mindedly to the opposing position (Tjosvold and D. Johnson 1978). The occurrence of controversy within a competitive context creates a closed-minded orientation in which individuals feel unwilling to make concessions to the opponent's viewpoint and closed-mindedly refuse to incorporate any of it into their own position. Within a competitive context, the increased understanding resulting from controversy tends to be ignored for a defensive adherence to one's own position. When individuals are unsure of the correctness of their position, they elect to be exposed to disconfirming information when it can easily be refuted, presumably because such refutation could affirm their own beliefs (Kleinhesselink and Edwards 1975;

Lowin 1969). Individuals elect to discuss an issue with a peer with an opposing position more frequently when the context is cooperative rather than competitive, and individuals in a competitive situation more often select a less competent peer to discuss an issue with (Van Blerkom and Tjosvold 1981). When the context is competitive, participants in a controversy understand but do not use others' information and ideas, but when the context is cooperative, they use the information and ideas provided by opponents (Tjosvold 1982; Tjosvold and Deemer 1980).

In addition to whether a cooperative or competitive climate dominates the situation, the skill with which individuals disagree with each other also affects the degree to which opponents' reasoning is incorporated into one's own position. When individuals involved in a controversy have their personal competence disconfirmed by their opponent, a closed-minded rejection of the opponent's position, information, and reasoning results (Tjosvold, D. Johnson, and Fabrey 1980; Tjosvold, D. Johnson, and Lerner 1981). The amount of defensiveness generated influences the degree to which individuals incorporate the opponent's information and reasoning into the decision makers' position, even when they understand accurately their opponent's position.

Changing attitude and position. Involvement in a controversy tends to result in a change in attitude and position. Disagreements within a group have been found to provide a greater amount of information and variety of facts as well as a change in the salience of known information that, in turn, results in shifts of judgment (Anderson and Graesser 1976; Kaplan 1977; Kaplan and Miller 1977; Nijhof and Kommers 1982; Vinokur and Burnstein 1974). Controversy has promoted a greater change in attitude than concurrence seeking, the lack of controversy, and individualistic learning (D. Johnson and R. Johnson 1985; R. Johnson et al. 1985). The likelihood of an agreement requiring a change in position is highest when there are strong pro and con arguments followed by the development of qualifiers and reservations as ways of finding an acceptable consensus (Putnam and Geist 1985).

Changing from one stage of cognitive reasoning to another. Cognitive development theorists (Flavell 1963; Kohlberg 1969; Piaget 1948, 1950) have posited that it is repeated interpersonal controversies (in which individuals are forced again and again to become aware of others' perspectives) that promote cognitive and moral development, the ability to think logically, and the reduction of egocentric reasoning. Such interpersonal conflicts are assumed to create disequilibrium within individuals' cognitive structures, motivating a search for a more adequate and mature process of reasoning. Researchers have paired preoperational children with operational peers and had them argue until they came to an agreement or stalemate about the solutions to various problems (F. Murray 1972; Silverman and Stone 1972). When tested alone after the interaction, 80 to 94 percent of the lower-level pupils gained significantly in performance compared to the very much lower rates of success reported in studies of more traditional training attempts (Beilin 1977; F. Murray 1978). In one case, eight out of 15 children who scored 0 out of 12 on the pretest had scores of 11 or 12 out of 12 on the various post-tests (F. Murray 1972).

Several studies have demonstrated that pairing a conserver with a nonconserver and giving the pair conservation problems to solve, instructing them to argue until they agree or reach a stalemate, results in the conserver's answer prevailing on the great majority of conservation trials and in the nonconserver's learning how to conserve (Ames and Murray 1982; Botvin and Murray 1975; Doise and Mugny 1979; Doise, Mugny, and Perret-Clermont 1976; Knight-Arest and Reid 1977; Miller and Brownell 1975; Mugny and Doise 1978; F. Murray 1972; F. Murray, Ames, and Botvin 1977; Perret-Clermont 1980; Silverman and Geiringer 1973; Silverman and Stone 1972; Smedslund 1961a, 1961b). In other studies, individuals (two-thirds of whom were nonconservers) who were placed in small groups, given a conservation task, and argued among themselves gave more adequate and higher-level explanations than did the control subjects who did not argue with one another (Inagaki 1981; Inagaki and Hatano 1968, 1977). Experimental subjects showed greater progress in generalizing the principle of conservation to a variety of situations and tended to resist extinction more often when they were shown an apparently nonconserving event. The discussion per se did not produce the effects: Conflict among individuals' explanations had to be present for the effects to appear.

The impact of controversy on cognitive and moral reasoning has been found in pairs (Silverman and Geiringer 1973;

Silverman and Stone 1972), two on one (F. Murray 1972), and three on two (Botvin and Murray 1975); in kindergarten, first, second, third, and fifth grades with normal and learning-disabled children (although not with those disabled by communication disorders) (Knight-Arest and Reid 1977); with African-Americans and whites; and with middle and low socioeconomic groups. Some researchers, however, did not find social interaction to be especially effective with mentally retarded institutionalized adolescents (IQ = 66, mental age = 10 years, chronological age = 20 years) (Borys and Spitz 1979). Agreement was often reached quickly. Nearly half the agreements were reached in less than 50 seconds and rarely took longer than four or five minutes (Miller and Brownell 1975). The advanced children did not prevail because of any greater social influence or higher IQ or because they were more skillful arguers. In arguments about concepts that have no developmental or necessity attributes, the advanced children won only 41 of 90 arguments, lost 38, and stalemated 11 (Miller and Brownell 1975). The advanced children seemed to initiate discussion slightly more often, stated their answer slightly more often, gave good reasons, countered the others slightly more often, moved stimuli more often, and appeared slightly more flexible in their arguments than did the immature children, who tended to repetitiously focus on their original opinion and its justifications (Miller and Brownell 1975; Silverman and Stone 1972). Growth tended to occur only for the children who yielded, which they did 60 to 80 percent of the time (Silverman and Geiringer 1973). Growth tended to occur through actual insight, not through parroting the answers of the advanced peers (Botvin and Murray 1975; Doise, Mugny, and Perret-Clermont 1976; Gelman 1978; F. Murray 1981). Change tended to be unidirectional and nonreversible. Children who understood conservation did not adopt erroneous strategies, while nonconservers tended to advance toward a greater understanding of conservation (Miller and Brownell 1975; Silverman and Geiringer 1973). Even two immature children who argued erroneous positions about the answer tended to make modest but significant gains toward an understanding of conservation (Ames and Murray 1982).

Similar studies have been conducted on moral reasoning. Typically, an individual who used lower-level moral reasoning to resolve a moral dilemma was placed in a cooperative pair with a peer who used a higher-level strategy, and the two were given the assignment of making a joint decision as to how a moral dilemma should be resolved. A controversy inevitably resulted. The studies using this procedure found that it tends to result in initially immature individuals' increasing their level of moral reasoning (Blatt 1969; Blatt and Kohlberg 1973; Crockenberg and Nicolayev 1977; Keasey 1973; Kuhn, Langer, Kohlberg, and Haan 1977; LeFurgy and Woloshin 1969; Maitland and Goldman 1974; Rest, Turiel, and Kohlberg 1969; Turiel 1966).

Taken together, these studies provide evidence that controversies among individuals promote transitions to higher stages of cognitive and moral reasoning. Such findings are important, as there is little doubt that higher levels of cognitive and moral reasoning cannot be directly taught (Inhelder and Sinclair 1969; Sigel and Hooper 1968; Sinclair 1969; Smedslund 1961a, 1961b; Turiel 1973; Wallach and Sprott 1964; Wallach, Wall, and Anderson 1967; Woholwill and Lowe 1962).

Summary. Students arrive at a synthesis by using higher-level thinking and reasoning, critically analyzing information, and using both deductive and inductive reasoning. Synthesis requires that students keep conclusions tentative, accurately understand opposing perspectives, incorporate new information into their conceptual frameworks, change their attitudes and positions, and use higher levels of cognitive and moral reasoning.

Conditions Mediating the Effects of Controversy

Although controversies can be beneficial, they will not be so under all conditions. As with all types of conflicts, the potential for either constructive or destructive outcomes is present in a controversy. Whether the consequences are positive or negative depends on the conditions under which controversy occurs and the way in which it is managed. These conditions and procedures include the goal structure within which the controversy occurs, participants' heterogeneity, the amount of relevant information distributed among participants, and participants' social skills.

A cooperative goal structure

The context in which conflicts occur has important effects on whether the conflict turns out to be constructive or destructive. Two contexts are possible for controversy: cooperative and competitive. A cooperative context facilitates constructive controversy, while a competitive context promotes destructive controversy in several ways (D. Johnson and R. Johnson 1983):

1. For controversy to be constructive, information must be accurately communicated. The communication of information is far more complete, accurate, encouraged, and used in a cooperative context than in a competitive context (D. Johnson 1974).
2. Constructive controversy requires a supportive climate in which group members feel safe enough to challenge each other's ideas. Cooperation provides a far more supportive climate than competition (D. Johnson and F. Johnson 1997).
3. For controversy to be constructive, it must be valued. Cooperative experiences promote stronger beliefs that controversy is valid and valuable (D. Johnson, R. Johnson, and Scott 1978; Lowry and D. Johnson 1981; Smith, D. Johnson, and R. Johnson 1981).
4. Constructive controversy requires dealing with feelings as well as with ideas and information. Evidence suggests that cooperativeness is positively related and competitiveness is negatively related to the ability to understand what others are feeling and why they are feeling that way (D. Johnson 1971a, 1975a, 1975b).
5. How controversies are defined has a great impact on how constructively they are managed. In a competitive context, controversies tend to be defined as win-lose situations (Deutsch 1973).
6. Constructive controversy requires a recognition of similarities and differences between positions. Group members participating in a controversy in a cooperative context identify more of the similarities between their positions than do members participating in a controversy in a competitive context (Judd 1978).

A cooperative context facilitates constructive controversy, while a competitive context promotes destructive controversy in several ways.

Evidence supports the argument that a cooperative context aids constructive controversy. In a cooperative context, individuals listen more open-mindedly to the opposing position (Tjosvold and D. Johnson 1978). Controversy in a competitive context, in contrast, creates a closed-minded orientation in which individuals comparatively feel unwilling to make concessions to the opponent's viewpoint and refuse to incorporate any of it into their own position. In a competitive context, the increased understanding that results from controversy tends to be ignored for a defensive adherence to one's own position. Participants in a controversy in a cooperative context seek out individuals with opposing opinions to test the validity of their ideas and reap the benefits of controversy, while participants in a controversy in a competitive context attempt to strengthen their opinions by choosing a more competent partner with the same opinion or a less competent discussant with an opposing view (Van Blerkom and Tjosvold 1981). Controversy in a cooperative context induces feelings of comfort, pleasure, and helpfulness in discussing opposing opinions; expectations of the other person's being helpful; feelings of trust and generosity toward the opponent; uncertainty about the correctness of the opponent's position; motivation to hear more about the opponent's arguments; a more accurate understanding of the opponent's position; and the reaching of more integrated positions where both one's own and the opponent's conclusions and reasoning are synthesized into a final position (Tjosvold 1982; Tjosvold and Deemer 1980). Controversy in a competitive context promotes closed-minded disinterest and rejection of the opponent's ideas and information. Avoidance of controversy results in little interest in or actual knowledge of opposing ideas and information and the making of a decision that reflects one's own views only. In a competitive context, however, when individuals are unsure of the correctness of their position, they select to be exposed to disconfirming information when it can easily be refuted, presumably because such refutation could affirm their own beliefs (Kleinhesselink and Edwards 1975; Lowin 1969).

Heterogeneity among members

Differences among individuals in personality, gender, attitudes, background, social class, reasoning strategies, cognitive perspectives, information, ability levels, and skills lead to diverse organization and processing of information and experiences, which, in turn, begins the cycle of controversy. Such differences have been found to promote achievement and productivity (Fiedler, Meuwese, and Oonk 1961; Frick 1973; D. Johnson 1977; Torrance 1961; Webb 1977). The greater the heterogeneity among individuals, the greater the amount of time spent in arguing (Nijhof and Kommers 1982). Heterogeneity among individuals leads to potential controversy and to more diverse interaction patterns and resources for achievement and problem solving.

Distribution of information
If controversy is to lead to achievement, individuals must possess information relevant to the completion of the tasks on which they are working. The more information individuals have about an issue, the greater their achievement and successful problem solving tend to be (Goldman 1965; Laughlin, Branch, and H. Johnson 1969). Having relevant information available, however, does not mean it will be used. Individuals need the interpersonal and group skills necessary to ensure that all individuals involved contribute their relevant information and that the information is synthesized effectively (Hall and Williams 1966; D. Johnson 1977).

Skilled disagreement
Controversy requires a complex set of procedures and skills that take some time to master. When unskilled individuals who have no previous experience with the process of controversy are required to engage in it, no advantage is expected. A comparison of the effectiveness of the presence and absence of controversy and systematic evaluation on the quality of decision making, for example, randomly assigned 154 graduate and undergraduate students at the University of Minnesota to the four conditions and to groups from four to seven members within the conditions (Lund 1980). The subjects, none of whom had previously participated in a structured controversy, participated in a one-hour experimental session in which they were instructed to follow the procedure of controversy or concurrence seeking or vigilant or nonvigilant decision-making behaviors. No significant differences in quality of decision making were found, and the conclusion was that the one-hour time limit was too short for subjects to learn the procedures of controversy and skillfully engage in them.

For controversies to be managed constructively, individuals need a number of collaborative and conflict management skills (D. Johnson and F. Johnson 1997; D. Johnson, R. Johnson, and Holubec 1993b). One of the most important is to be able to disagree with each other's ideas while confirming each other's personal competence. Disagreeing with others while at the same time imputing that they are incompetent tends to increase their commitment to their own ideas and their rejection of the others' information and reasoning (Tjosvold 1974). When individuals involved in a controversy have their personal competence disconfirmed by their opponent, the result is a closed-minded rejection of the opponent's position, information, and reasoning (Tjosvold, D. Johnson, and Fabrey 1980; Tjosvold, D. Johnson, and Lerner 1981). The amount of defensiveness generated influences the degree to which individuals incorporate the opponent's information and reasoning into their position, even when they understand accurately their opponent's position. Disagreeing with others while simultaneously confirming their personal competence, however, results in being better liked and in the opponents' being less critical of one's ideas, more interested in learning more about one's ideas, and more willing to incorporate one's information and reasoning into their own analysis of the problem (Tjosvold, D. Johnson, and Fabrey 1980; Tjosvold, D. Johnson, and Lerner 1981).

Another important set of skills for exchanging information and opinions in a controversy is *perspective taking*. More information, both personal and impersonal, is disclosed when one is interacting with a person engaging in perspective-taking behaviors, such as paraphrasing to demonstrate understanding and to communicate the desire to understand accurately. Perspective taking increases one's capacity to phrase messages so that others easily understand them and to comprehend accurately others' messages. Engaging in perspective taking in conflict situations tends to increase understanding and retention of the opponent's information and perspective, facilitate the achievement of creative, high-quality problem solving, and promote more positive perceptions of the process of exchanging information, fellow group members, and the group's work (Falk and D. Johnson 1977; D. Johnson 1971a, 1977). The greater the clarity of group members' understanding of all sides of the issues and the more accurate the assessment of their validity and relative merits, the more creative the synthesis of all positions in a controversy tends to be.

Summary
It is not enough to know that academic controversies result in increased achievement and retention, higher-quality prob-

lem solving and decision making, more frequent creative insight, a more thorough exchange of expertise, greater task involvement, closer and more positive relationships, and greater social competence and self-esteem. We must also understand the process by which they do so. The process consists of giving individuals a problem to solve on which they arrive at an initial conclusion, having individuals present their conclusion and its rationale to others, confronting individuals with other conclusions that create uncertainty characterized by cognitive conflict or disequilibrium, actively searching for more information and a more adequate cognitive perspective and reasoning process, and synthesizing a new conclusion by adapting cognitive perspectives and accommodating the perspective and reasoning of others. Controversies tend to be constructive when the context is cooperative, group members are somewhat heterogeneous, information and expertise are distributed within the group, and members have the necessary skills in resolving conflicts. While the controversy process sometimes occurs naturally in cooperative learning groups, it can be considerably enhanced when faculty structure academic controversies.

THE INSTRUCTOR'S ROLE IN STRUCTURING ACADEMIC CONTROVERSIES

Conflict is the gadfly of thought. It stirs us to observation and memory. It instigates invention. It shocks us out of sheeplike passivity, and sets us at noting and contriving. . . . Conflict is a "sine qua non" of reflection and ingenuity.

—John Dewey

"Are wolves a national treasure that should be allowed to roam free while being protected from hunting and trapping? Or are wolves a renewable resource that should be managed for sport and revenue? Ecologists say that wolves should be a protected species. But many farmers, ranchers, and sportsmen believe that wolves should be managed. What do you think? Can you prove you are right?" An ecology instructor asks her class to take a stand on the wolf. "You," she says to the class, "must write a report explaining what should happen to the wolf in the continental United States and why. To ensure that the reports represent your best thinking, you will write it cooperatively with several of your classmates." She then randomly assigns students to heterogeneous groups of four and divides each group into two pairs. One pair is assigned the position that wolves should be a protected species, the other that wolves should be a managed species.

This instructor has prepared the way for structuring an academic controversy, choosing a topic that has content students can manage and on which at least two well-documented positions (pro and con) can be prepared, structuring cooperative learning by assigning students to learning groups of four, creating resource interdependence by giving each pair half of the materials, and highlighting the cooperative goals of reaching a consensus on the issue, writing a group report on which all members will be evaluated, and preparing each member to take a test on the information studied. She is now ready to conduct the controversy, which involves a structured and complex process (figure 2).

Creating a Cooperative Context
The first step in managing conflict effectively is to establish a constructive context. The context within which conflicts occur largely determines whether the conflict is managed constructively or destructively (Deutsch 1973; D. Johnson and R. Johnson 1989; Tjosvold and D. Johnson 1983; Watson

and D. Johnson 1972). Two contexts are possible: cooperative and competitive (in individualistic situations, individuals
do not interact and, therefore, no conflict occurs).

FIGURE 2

The Teacher's Role in Structuring Academic Controversies

The Context for Conflict

- Competitive context
- Cooperative context

Cooperative Learning

- Positive interdependence
- Individual accountability
- Face-to-face promotive interaction
- Social skills
- Group processing

The Teacher's Role

➤ *Step 1: Preinstructional Decisions and Preparation*

- Set objectives and select topic
- Decide on size of group
- Assign students to groups
- Arrange the room
- Plan instructional materials
- Assign roles

➤ *Step 2: Orchestrating Academic Task, Cooperative Structure, Controversy Procedure*

- Explain academic task
- Structure positive interdependence
- Structure the controversy
- Structure individual accountability
- Explain criteria for success
- Specify desired behaviors

➤ *Step 3: Monitoring and Intervening*

- Observe interaction among group members
- Ensure adherence to controversy procedures
- Provide academic assistance
- Teach controversy skills

➤ *Step 4: Evaluating and Processing*

- Provide closure
- Assess and evaluate students' learning
- Process how well the group did
- Celebrate as a group

Competitive context
Conflicts usually do not go well in a competitive context. Competition exists when students work against each other to achieve a goal that only one or a few students can attain. Although competition may enhance achievement in certain limited conditions (D. Johnson and R. Johnson 1994b), individuals in competitive situations typically have a short-term time orientation where all energies are focused on winning. Little or no attention is paid to maintaining a good relationship. In competitive situations:

1. Communication tends to be avoided, but when it does occur, it tends to contain misleading information, threats, personal attacks, espionage to obtain information about the other that the other is unwilling to communicate, and diversionary tactics to delude or mislead the opponent.
2. Misperceptions and distortions of the other person's position and motivations that are difficult to correct are common and frequent. Students engage in self-fulfilling prophecies by perceiving another person as immoral and hostile and behaving accordingly, thus evoking hostility and deceit from the other person. Students see opponents' small misbehaviors while ignoring their own large misbehaviors (the mote-beam mechanism). Double standards exist. The misperceptions are difficult to correct because preconceptions and expectations influence what is perceived, a bias exists toward seeing events in a way that justifies one's own beliefs and actions, and conflict and threats impair perceptual and cognitive processes.
3. Individuals have a suspicious, hostile attitude toward each other that increases their readiness to exploit each other's wants and needs and refuse each other's requests.
4. Individuals tend to deny the legitimacy of others' wants, needs, and feelings and consider only their own interests (Deutsch 1973; D. Johnson and R. Johnson 1989; Tjosvold and D. Johnson 1983; Watson and D. Johnson 1972).

Cooperative context
Conflicts usually go well in a cooperative context. In such situations, individuals typically have a long-term time orientation where they focus their energies on achieving goals and on building good working relationships with others (Deutsch 1973; D. Johnson and R. Johnson 1989; Tjosvold

and D. Johnson 1983; Watson and D. Johnson 1972). In co-operative situations, the communication of relevant information tends to be more frequent, complete, and accurate; perceptions of the other person and the other person's actions are far more accurate and constructive; individuals trust and like each other; and conflicts tend to be defined as mutual problems to be solved in ways that benefit everyone involved. To use academic controversies effectively, an instructor first has to establish a cooperative context, primarily through the use of cooperative learning. (See D. Johnson, R. Johnson, and Smith [1991] for a complete and thorough discussion of cooperative learning.)

When lessons are structured cooperatively, students work together to accomplish shared goals. Cooperative learning involves far more than a seating arrangement, however. Seating students together can result in competition at close quarters or individualistic efforts with talking. Simply placing students in groups and telling them to work together does not in and of itself result in cooperative efforts. It is only when five basic elements are carefully structured in a group that the group is cooperative:

1. *Positive interdependence.* Positive interdependence is the perception that you are linked with others in such a way that you cannot succeed unless they do (and vice versa); that is, their work benefits you and your work benefits them. During every cooperative lesson, positive goal interdependence must be established through *mutual learning goals* (learn the assigned material and make sure that all members of your group learn the assigned material), which may be supplemented by *joint rewards* (if all members of your group score 90 percent correct or better on the test, each will receive five bonus points); *divided resources* (giving each group member a part of the total information required to complete an assignment) and *complementary roles* (reader, checker, encourager, elaborator) may also be used.
2. *Individual accountability.* Individual accountability exists when the performance of each student is assessed and the results given back to the group and the individual. Common ways to structure individual accountability include giving an individual test to each student, randomly selecting one student's product to represent the

Simply placing students in groups and telling them to work together does not in and of itself result in cooperative efforts.

entire group, or having each student explain what he or she has learned to a classmate.

3. *Face-to-face promotive interaction.* Students promote each other's success by helping, assisting, supporting, encouraging, and praising each other's efforts to learn. Certain cognitive activities and interpersonal dynamics occur only when students explain how to solve problems, discuss the nature of the concepts being learned, teach their knowledge to classmates, and connect present with past learning. Accountability to peers, ability to influence each other's reasoning and conclusions, social modeling, social support, and interpersonal rewards all increase as the face-to-face interaction among group members increases.

4. *Social skills.* Contributing to the success of a cooperative effort requires interpersonal and small-group skills. Students must be taught the social skills for high-quality cooperation and be motivated to use them. Leadership, decision-making, trust-building, communication, and conflict-management skills must be taught just as purposefully and precisely as academic skills. (See D. Johnson [1991, 1997] and D. Johnson and F. Johnson [1997] for procedures and strategies for teaching students social skills.)

5. *Group processing.* Group processing exists when group members discuss how well they are achieving their goals and maintaining effective working relationships. Groups need to describe which actions of the members are helpful and which are not and decide which behaviors to continue or change (D. Johnson and R. Johnson 1989; D. Johnson, R. Johnson, and Smith 1991).

Because academic controversies take place in cooperative learning groups, each of these basic elements must be carefully structured when faculty create an academic controversy.

Using Academic Controversies

To conduct an academic controversy, instructors:

1. Make a number of decisions before instruction actually begins.
2. Clearly explain the task, the positive interdependence, and the procedure for controversy to students.

3. Monitor the effectiveness of cooperative learning groups and intervene as necessary to provide assistance in completing the task, following the procedure for controversy, or using the required interpersonal and group skills.
4. Assess and evaluate students' achievement and help students process how well they functioned as a group.

Preinstructional decisions and preparations
Specifying the objectives and topic. An instructor needs to specify two types of objectives before the lesson begins. The *academic objective* must be specified at the correct level for students and matched to the right level of instruction according to a conceptual or task analysis. The *social skills objective* details what interpersonal and small-group skills will be emphasized during the lesson. A common error many instructors make is to specify only academic objectives and ignore the social skills needed to train students to cooperate and disagree constructively with each other.

In specifying objectives, the instructor chooses a topic for the controversy, making sure that at least two well-documented positions can be prepared and that students can manage the content. Almost any issue being studied can be turned into a controversy. The instructor should also keep in mind that whenever students work together in cooperative learning groups, natural controversies will arise during the course of their making decisions and solving problems. By participating in structured academic controversies, students will learn the procedures and skills to use when unplanned, natural controversies suddenly arise.

Deciding on the size of groups. Unless you plan to use an observer, cooperative learning groups of four should be used for structured controversies. Each position usually has two students assigned to work as a team in preparations to advocate it. While some issues might lend themselves to three positions (and thus to groups of six), the complexity of synthesizing three positions and managing the interaction among six students is such that groups are typically limited to four. The more inexperienced students are in working cooperatively and engaging in controversy, the shorter the class period, and the more limited the materials, the more the size of the group should definitely be limited to four.

Assigning students to groups. To increase the potential for controversy, the heterogeneity of students within each learning group should be maximized so that students of different achievement levels in math, ethnic backgrounds, genders, and social classes work together. The heterogeneity among group members increases the likelihood that different perspectives and viewpoints will naturally occur. In addition, heterogeneity among students typically increases performance in solving problems and learning concepts. When in doubt about how to maximize heterogeneity, randomly assign students to groups.

Arranging the room. Members of a learning group should sit close enough to each other so that they can share materials, talk to each other quietly, and maintain eye contact with all group members. Circles are usually best. The instructor should have clear access lanes to every group. Students will have to move into pairs and then back into groups of four.

Planning instructional materials to promote interdependence and controversy. Divide materials to be used for the controversies into pro and con positions so that each pair of students has part of the materials needed to complete the task. The following materials typically are needed for each position:

1. A clear description of the group's task.
2. A description of the phases of the controversy procedure and the collaborative skills to be used during each phase.
3. A definition of the position to be advocated with a summary of the key arguments supporting the position.
4. A set of resource materials (including a bibliography) to provide evidence for and elaboration of the arguments supporting the position to be advocated.

The presentation should be balanced for all sides of the controversy, and the materials should be separated into packets containing articles, reports, or summaries supporting each position on the issue.

Assigning roles. Inherent in the procedure for an academic controversy is assigning students to a pro or con advocacy pair. In effect, this step involves assigning students complementary roles that signal their positive interdependence within the procedure. Instructors might also wish to assign students other roles related to working together cooperatively and engaging in intellectual arguments.

Explaining and orchestrating the academic task, cooperative goal structure, and controversy procedure

Explaining the academic task. Instructors must explain the academic task so that students are clear about the assignment and understand the objectives of the lesson. Instructors may directly teach concepts, principles, and strategies at this point. They may wish to answer any questions students have about the concepts or facts they are to learn or apply in the lesson. In addition to explaining the procedure, instructors may help students immerse themselves in the role by presenting the issue to be decided as interestingly and dramatically as possible. In any event, the task must be structured so that it involves at least two well-documented positions. The choice of topic depends on the instructor's interests and the purposes of the course.

Structuring positive interdependence. Instructors must communicate to students that they have a group goal and must work cooperatively. A controversy has two goals for the group:

1. To produce a single report and arrive at a consensus about the decision. Students are responsible for ensuring that all group members participate in writing a quality report for the group and presenting the information to the class.
2. To ensure that all group members master all the information relevant to both sides of the issue (as measured by a test that each student takes individually). Students are responsible for group members' knowing the information.

To supplement the effects of positive goal interdependence, the materials are distributed so that each member receives *part* of the total information required to complete the task (*resource interdependence*). Bonus points may be given if *all* group members score above a certain criterion on the test (*reward interdependence*).

Structuring the controversy. The principal prerequisites for a successful structured controversy are a cooperative context, skillful group members, and the group's heterogeneity. The cooperative context is established by:

1. Assigning students to heterogeneous groups of four and dividing each group into two pairs. A good reader and a poor reader may be assigned to each pair. Each pair is responsible for learning the information supporting its assigned position and preparing a presentation and a series of persuasive arguments to use in the discussion with the opposing pair.
2. Assigning pro and con positions to the pairs and giving students supporting materials to read and study. Students may also be given a bibliography of further sources of information. A section of resource materials may be set up in the library.
3. Structuring positive interdependence.

Students will need to be taught the necessary skills in conflict management. The skills may be taught simultaneously with students' participating in structured controversies. The group's heterogeneity adds to the resources and the perspectives that can contribute to spirited and constructive arguments, increasing the quality of the structured controversy.

More specifically, a controversy involves five stages:

1. *Learning positions.* Meet with your partner and plan how to advocate your position effectively. Read the materials supporting your position. Find more information in the library and in reference books to support your position. Give the opposing pair any information found supporting the opposing position. Prepare a persuasive presentation to be given to the other pair. Prepare a series of persuasive arguments to be used in the discussion with the opposing pair. Plan with your partner how to advocate your position effectively. Make sure you and your partner master the information supporting your assigned position and present it persuasively and completely so that the other group members will comprehend and learn the information.
2. *Presenting positions.* Present the best case for your position to ensure it gets a fair and complete hearing. Be

The group's hetero- geneity adds to the resources and the perspec- tives that can con- tribute to spirited and con- structive arguments, increasing the quality of the structured contro- versy.

forceful and persuasive in doing so. Use more than one medium. Listen carefully to and learn the opposing position. Take notes and clarify anything you do not understand.

3. *Discussing the issue (advocating, refuting, rebutting).* Openly discuss the issue by freely exchanging information and ideas. Argue forcefully and persuasively for your position, presenting as many facts as you can to support your point of view. Listen critically to the opposing pair's evidence and reasoning, probe and push the opposing pair's thinking, ask for data to support assertions, and then present counterarguments. Defend your position. Compare the strengths and weaknesses of the two positions. Refute the claims being made by the opposing pair, and rebut the attacks on your position. Follow the specific rules for constructive controversy. Take careful notes on and thoroughly learn the opposing position. Sometimes a "time-out" period will be provided so you can caucus with your partner and prepare new arguments. Your instructor may encourage more spirited arguing, take sides when a pair is in trouble, play devil's advocate, ask one group to observe another group engaging in a spirited argument, and generally stir up the discussions. Remember, this issue is complex, and you need to know both sides to write a good report. Make sure you understand the facts that support both points of view.

4. *Reversing perspectives.* Change chairs with the other pair. Present the opposing pair's position as if you were they. Use your notes to do so. Be as sincere and forceful as you can. Add any new facts you know of. Elaborate their position by relating it to other information you previously learned.

5. *Reaching a decision.* Drop your advocacy of your assigned position. Summarize and synthesize the best arguments for both points of view. Reach a consensus on a position that is supported by the facts. Change your mind only when the facts and rationale clearly indicate you should do so.

Write a group report with the supporting evidence and rationale for the synthesis your group has agreed on. Often the resulting position is a third perspective or synthesis that is more rational than the two assigned. All group members sign the report when it is as good as they can make it, indicating that they agree with it, can explain its content, and consider it ready to be evaluated. Organize your report to present it to your entire class.

Take a test on both positions. If all members score above the predetermined criterion for excellence, each one receives five bonus points.

Process how well the group functioned and how its performance can be improved during the next controversy. Instructors may wish to structure the group processing to highlight the specific conflict management skills students need to master.

Structuring individual accountability. The purpose of the controversy is to make each group member a stronger individual; therefore, the level of each student's learning must be assessed. Individual accountability is structured by individually testing each student on the material studied and/or randomly choosing one member of each group to present his or her group's decision and its rationale to the class as a whole. Students should also be observed to ensure that each one participates in each step of the procedure.

Explaining the criteria for success. Evaluations of cooperatively structured lessons (and controversies are no exception) must be related to specific criteria. At the beginning of the lesson, instructors must explain clearly the criteria by which students' work will be evaluated.

Specifying desired behaviors. No matter how carefully instructors structure a controversy, the controversy does not produce its potential effects if students do not have the interpersonal and small-group skills to manage conflicts constructively. The social skills emphasized are those involved in systematically advocating an intellectual position and evaluating and criticizing the position advocated by others, as well as the skills involved in synthesis and consensual decision making. Students should be taught several skills:

1. How to emphasize the mutuality of the situation and avoid win-lose dynamics; how to focus on coming to the best decision possible, not on winning.
2. How to confirm others' competence while disagreeing with their positions and challenging their reasoning.

How to be critical of ideas, not people. How to challenge and refute the ideas of the members of the opposing pair without rejecting them personally.

3. How to separate your personal worth from criticism of your ideas.

4. How to listen to everyone's ideas, even if you do not agree with them.

5. How to first bring out all the ideas and facts supporting both sides and then try to put them together in a way that makes sense. How to be able to differentiate positions before attempting to integrate ideas.

6. How to take the opposing perspective to understand the opposing position. How to try to understand both sides of the issue.

7. How to change your mind when the evidence clearly indicates that you should.

8. How to paraphrase what someone has said if it is not clear.

9. How to emphasize rationality in seeking the best possible answer, given the available data.

10. How to follow the golden rule of conflict—act toward your opponents as you would have them act toward you. How to understand that if you want people to listen to you, then you must listen to them; that if you want others to include your ideas in their thinking, then you must include their ideas in your thinking; that if you want others to take your perspective, then you must take their perspective.

Structuring intergroup cooperation. When preparing their positions, students can check with classmates in other groups who are also preparing the same position, sharing ideas as to how best to present and advocate the position. If one pair of students finds information that supports its position, members can share that information with other pairs who have the same position. The more conferring between pairs of students, the better. The positive outcomes found with a cooperative learning group can be extended throughout a whole class by structuring intergroup cooperation. Bonus points may be given if all members of a class reach a preset criterion of excellence. When a group finishes its work, the instructor should encourage the members to help other groups complete the assignment.

Monitoring and intervening

Monitoring students' behavior. Instructors should observe group members to see what problems they are having completing the assignment and skillfully engaging in controversy. Whenever possible, instructors should use a formal observation sheet to count the number of times they observe students using appropriate behaviors. The more concrete the data, the more useful it is to the instructor and to students. Instructors should not try to count too many different behaviors at one time, especially when they first start formal observation. At first, they may want just to keep track of who talks in each group (see D. Johnson and R. Johnson [1994b] for a description of systematic observation of cooperative groups), but behaviors that could be monitored include contributing ideas, asking questions, expressing feelings, listening actively, expressing support for and acceptance of ideas, expressing warmth and liking toward group members and the group, encouraging all members to participate, summarizing, checking for understanding, relieving tension by joking, and giving direction to the group's work. All these behaviors are positive behaviors, which are to be praised when they are appropriately present and are a cause for discussion when they are missing. It is also a good idea for the instructor to collect notes on students' specific behaviors so that he or she can keep track of the frequency with which certain behaviors occur. Especially useful are skillful interchanges that can be shared with students later as objective praise.

Providing academic assistance. In monitoring the learning groups as they work, instructors will wish to clarify instructions, review important concepts and strategies, answer questions, and teach academic skills as necessary. Students may need assistance at any stage of the process, whether it is researching their position, advocating it, refuting the opposing position, defending their position from attack, reversing perspectives, or creatively synthesizing a position.

Intervening to teach controversy skills. While monitoring learning groups, instructors will often find students who do not have the necessary skills in resolving conflict and groups whose members are having problems disagreeing effectively. In these cases, instructors should intervene to suggest more effective procedures for working together and more effective behaviors. They may wish to teach directly basic interpersonal and small-group skills (D. Johnson 1997; D. Johnson and F. Johnson 1997), and they may also wish to intervene and reinforce particularly effective and skillful behaviors that they notice. At times, the instructor becomes a consultant to a group to help it function more effectively.

The best time to teach controversy skills is when the students need them. Intervening should leave group members with new skills that will be useful in the future. At a minimum:

1. Students need to recognize the need for the skill.
2. The skill must be defined clearly and specifically, including what students should say when engaging in the skill.
3. Practicing the skill must be encouraged. Sometimes just the instructor's standing there with a clipboard and pencil will be enough to promote students' enactment of the skill.
4. Students should have the time to discuss how well they are using the skills. Students should persevere in the practice until they internalize the skill. One never drops a skill, only adds to it.

Evaluating and processing

Providing closure to the lesson. At the end of each instructional unit, students should be able to summarize what they have learned. The instructor may wish to summarize the major points in the lesson, ask students to recall ideas or give examples, and answer any final questions students have.

Evaluating students' learning. Instructors evaluate students' work, assess their learning, and provide feedback about how their work compares with the criteria of excellence established. The instructor should address both qualitative and quantitative aspects of their performance. Students receive a group grade on the quality of their final report and an individual grade for their performance on the test covering both sides of the issue.

Processing how well the group functioned. When students have completed the assignment, they should describe what actions taken by the members were helpful (and unhelpful) in completing the group's work and decide what behaviors to continue or change. Group processing occurs at two levels—in each learning group and in the class as a whole. Processing for the small groups involves members' discussing how effectively they worked together and what could be improved. Processing for the whole class involves the instructor's giving the class feedback and having students share incidents that occurred in their groups. Feedback given to students should be descriptive and specific, not evaluative and general (see D. Johnson [1997]). If the learning groups are to function better tomorrow than they did today, students must receive feedback, reflect on how their actions could be more effective, and plan how to be even more skillful during the next group session.

Summary

The instructor's role in implementing structured academic controversies is an extension of the instructor's role in using cooperative learning. It consists of specifying the objectives for learning and social skills, making a number of decisions about preparation for the exercise, explaining and orchestrating the academic task and the controversy, monitoring students' performance and intervening if necessary, and evaluating and processing the lessons learned. Academic controversies can be used in any subject area with any age student. Yet implementing structured academic controversies is not easy. It can take years to become an expert. Instructors may wish to start small by taking one subject area or one class and using controversy until they feel comfortable, then expand into other subject areas or other classes. Instructors should choose topics for which they are fairly certain a controversy will work, plan carefully, and not rush the process. To implement academic controversies successfully, instructors will need to teach students the interpersonal and small-group skills required to cooperate, engage in intellectual inquiry, intellectually challenge each other, see a situation from several perspective simultaneously, and synthesize a variety of positions into a new and creative decision. Implementing academic controversies in the classroom may take some time and energy, but it is worth the effort.

In addition to understanding the instructor's overall role in conducting academic controversies, instructors must be able to manage each step of the procedure. The first step is to have students research their assigned position and prepare to advocate it.

The instructor's role in implementing structured academic controversies is an extension of the instructor's role in using cooperative learning.

HOW TO SOLVE IT: ANALYTICALLY OR NUMERICALLY?

Tasks: Your tasks are to (1) write a group report on when incoming engineering students should use analytical and numerical methods for solving mathematical expressions and (2) individually pass a test on the mathematics involved.

Two principal methods for solving mathematical expressions are analytical and numerical. *Analytical methods* use the principles of algebra and symbolic manipulation, *numerical methods* the power of computers (algorithms and iterative procedures) and approximation. Your group has been chosen to advise incoming students on the promises and pitfalls of each approach. You may assume that they have had calculus in high school and that they are familiar with a graphing calculator for performing numerical integration and differentiation. In writing your group report, apply the principles and strategies you have learned in your engineering and math courses to address this issue. The report should present both positions and provide details of the advantages and disadvantages of each procedure.

Cooperative: Write one report for the group of four. All members have to agree. Everyone has to be able to explain the choice made and the reasons the choice is a good one. To help you write the best report possible, your group of four has been divided into two pairs. One pair has been assigned the position that analytical methods are best, the other that numerical methods are best.

Procedure:

1. *Research and prepare your position.* Your group of four has been divided into two pairs. Each pair is to make a list of reasons supporting its position and plan how to present the best case for its position to the other pair.

2. *Present and advocate your position.* Forcefully and persuasively present the best case for your list to the opposing pair. Be as convincing as possible. Take notes and clarify anything you do not understand when the opposing pair presents its case.

3. *Open discussion (advocate, refute, rebut).* Argue forcefully and persuasively for your position. Critically evaluate and challenge the opposing pair's list and reasoning and defend your reasoning from attack.

4. *Reverse perspectives.* Reverse perspectives and present the best case for the opposing position. The opposing pair will do the same. Strive to see the issue from both perspectives simultaneously.

5. *Synthesize.* Drop all advocacy. Synthesize and integrate the best advice and reasoning from both sides into a joint position that all members can agree to. Then finalize the group report, present your conclusions to the class, ensure that all group members are prepared to take the test, and process how well you worked together as a group and how you could be even more effective next time.

PREPARING A POSITION

He that wrestles with us strengthens our nerves, and
sharpens our skill. Our antagonist is our helper.
                                        —Edmund Burke

In 1982, a B-737 crashed into the 14th Street Bridge in Washington, D.C., while taking off from National Airport. The crash was traced to a mechanical problem. The pilot, misled by an ice-jammed thrust indicator, had set the engine thrust too low to take off safely. But faulty group decision making also contributed to the crash. During the takeoff, the copilot noticed that the plane was not reacting properly, and he repeatedly advised the captain. The copilot's warnings, however, were so subtle that the captain ignored them. In 1978, a DC-8 crashed because the crew, while checking a malfunctioning instrument, ignored the plane's dangerously low level of fuel. The flight engineer reported the low fuel to the captain, but he dismissed the warning. The problem of poor decision making by the cockpit crew is significant, for it literally means life or death, not only for the crew, but also for the passengers on board. Estimates suggest that 65 to 80 percent of all airplane transport crashes that occurred in the United States between 1969 and 1979 resulted from faulty group decision making rather than mechanical problems. Poor decision making by the cockpit crew most often occurs when the crew members have no procedure for disagreeing with each other constructively.

Whether the organization is a business, an industry, a government agency, a hospital, a law firm, a family, or a school, people disagree with each other as decisions are made and problems are solved. In almost every meeting room in every organization, people disagree with each other. Involved participation in such situations means that different ideas, opinions, beliefs, and information surface and clash; that is, controversy occurs. Most groups waste the benefits of such disputes, but every effective decision-making situation thrives on what controversy has to offer. Decisions are by their very nature controversial, as alternative solutions are suggested and considered before agreement is reached. When a decision is made, the controversy ends and participants commit themselves to a common course of action.

Students, just like engineers, executives, politicians, and judges, have to decide how to solve problems in every class they take. Participating in academic controversies is just as powerful as (and wonderful preparation for) the controversies involved in decision making in business, industry, government, and other similar settings.

Preparing a Position

"Was the Boston Tea Party an act of heroic patriotism? Or was it a needless criminal act that did not help America achieve its freedom? What do you think? Convince me you are right." To harness the power of academic controversy, an instructor assigns students to groups of four and asks them to prepare a report on the Boston Tea Party. Each group is to prepare one report representing the members' best reasoned judgment about the issue. The instructor then divides the groups into two-person advocacy teams and assigns one team the position that the Boston Tea Party was an act of heroic patriotism, the other the position that it was a useless criminal act. Both teams are given articles and materials supporting their assigned position and then are given time to read and discuss the materials with their partner. They plan how best to advocate their assigned position so that they learn the information and perspective, convince the opposing team of the soundness of the team's position, and teach the members of the opposing team the material contained in the resources.

To engage in a controversy, students must:

1. *Research (look).* Gather evidence to support the assigned position.
2. *Conceptualize (think).* Organize the evidence into a logical structure that provides a rationale for the position.
3. *Leap to a conclusion.* Reach a tentative conclusion based on students' current understanding of the issue.
4. *Present (tell).* Plan how to advocate the position forcefully and persuasively (figure 3).

As they research, conceptualize, conclude, and tell, students seek as complete an intellectual understanding of the issue as current knowledge allows while using a set of social and cognitive skills to solve the problem.

FIGURE 3

Preparing a Position

RESEARCHING
- Gather text and course materials
- Use library and computer searches
- Categorize results into supportive and nonsupportive
- Categorize supporting evidence into most, moderately, and least important
- Differentiate between facts and beliefs
- Appeal to authority (not to longevity)

ORGANIZING
- Place information into a conceptual framework
- Arrange information in logical order through the combined use of inductive and deductive logic

LEAPING TO A CONCLUSION
- Decide what is known
- Decide what is unknown or yet to be discovered
- Draw a conclusion as to the validity and correctness of a thesis or claim on the basis of probabilities, not dualistic or relativist reasoning

PREPARING TO PRESENT YOUR POSITION
- Take the other perspective
- Use more than one modality
- Practice your presentation

Researching a position

Researching a position involves gathering and collecting all facts, information, experiences, and other evidence relevant to the assigned position. Students take their assigned thesis statement or claim and, working in pairs, engage in the following activities:

1. Read the textbook and the materials provided by the instructor.
2. Do library research to find facts, information, experiences, and other evidence to support the validity of your position. Search the library to find books and arti-

cles on the topic; use computer searches and interview knowledgeable individuals.

3. List resources, writing down all the information needed on an index card to include the resources in your bibliography.

4. List and detail the facts, information, experiences, and other evidence that relate to the thesis statement. List each piece of relevant information on an index card.

5. Sort the evidence into supporting and nonsupporting categories. Give all the nonsupporting evidence to the opposing pair.

6. Select the most important evidence to include in the rationale by dividing the information supporting the thesis statement into most, moderately, and least important and according to recency, quantity of evidence, quality of evidence, and consistency of evidence. The more recent the evidence, the greater the amount, the more reliable and valid it is, and the more consistent it is, the better.

Differentiating between fact and belief (opinion). In constructing the rationale for your position, stay as close as possible to the facts—which means you need to know the difference between fact and belief. Facts refer to things, states, or events that can be proved by experience. Facts can be verified by the senses (measuring, weighing, and counting, for example) or by inferences from physical data so strong as to allow no other explanation. Some facts are that Roger weighs 150 pounds, Edythe is over five feet tall, and Abraham Lincoln was president of the United States. Beliefs, on the other hand, are thought to be true but are beyond the reach of verification through our senses; that is, they cannot be measured, weighed, or counted. Many people believe that world peace is possible, that life exists on other planets, that Atlantis will someday be discovered, and that an earthquake will destroy Los Angeles. But none of these statements can be proved. Beliefs can be presented as part of a persuasive argument so long as you do not assume that you have proved them or that your beliefs prove your claim. In using beliefs as part of your argument, remember the medieval saying *De gustibus non est disputandum*—tastes are not to be disputed. You may believe that Chinese food tastes better than Italian food, but you should not argue about it.

Appealing to authority. In gathering your information, you are setting up an appeal to authority. First, you appeal to theory and research as the major authorities. What we now know is an important part of any controversy. Second, you appeal to the beliefs of great theorists or researchers as authorities.

An appeal to an authority to prove your point is actually an appeal beyond logic (but not necessarily beyond reason). "Freud said" can silence many an objection. Appeals to Einstein, Shakespeare, Eleanor Roosevelt, Adam Smith, or Gandhi can authenticate many a claim, as such people have often proved themselves to be right. Appeals to authority, however, risk four common fallacies, and the more eminent the authority, the easier it is to make one of the fallacies:

1. Appealing to an authority outside his or her field. Freud had a brilliant mind, but he did not know a great deal about mass media. Ask yourself whether you are citing the authority outside his or her field.
2. Misunderstanding or misrepresenting what the authority really said. Ask yourself whether you are presenting his or her views accurately.
3. Assuming that one quote from an authority represents his or her conclusions accurately. Ask yourself whether a particular instance really represents the authority's view.
4. Not knowing that the authority is outdated. Ask yourself whether the authority is still fully authoritative.

Appealing to the longevity of the conclusion. Related to appeals to authority are appeals to the longevity of a conclusion. You can say, "Because this belief has persisted, it must be true," but no one should agree with you. For hundreds of years, people believed the ancient Greek philosophers who concluded that the physical world contains four basic elements—air, earth, fire, and water. Because the belief lasted hundreds of years did not make it true.

Organizing what is known into a reasoned position
When the research is completed, the information must be organized into a persuasive argument. The aim of a persuasive argument is to lead listeners step by step from lack of knowledge to an informed conclusion that agrees with their

thesis statement. A persuasive argument begins with a thesis statement or claim and presents a rationale that leads the audience to a clearly defined conclusion that is the same as the thesis statement. Thus, a persuasive argument has three parts:

1. *A thesis statement* or *claim* that asserts something is true. It is a statement the arguer wants accepted but expects to be challenged, for example, "George Washington was the greatest president the United States has ever had." A thesis statement or claim often includes qualifiers and reservations. Qualifiers are ways of communicating how confident the speaker is about his or her claim and involve words like "probably," "sometimes," "never," and "always." Reservations are the circumstances under which the speaker would decide not to defend a claim and involve words like "unless" and "until."

2. *A rationale* that arranges the supporting facts, information, experiences, and other evidence into a coherent, reasoned, valid, and logical sequence leading the audience to the clearly defined conclusion that the claim is true. The proponent strives for solid evidence and sound reasoning. "Because George Washington militarily won our independence from England, was a unifying symbol for all 13 colonies, was the role model for subsequent presidents, and provided a stable government during our country's formative years, then. . . ."

3. *A conclusion* that is the same as the original thesis statement and is derived on the basis of principles of scientific inquiry and deductive and inductive logic. The facts are arranged, composed, and linked together in a logical structure that leads to the conclusion and thereby makes the case for the thesis statement. " . . . George Washington was therefore the greatest president the United States has ever had."

Students organize or conceptualize what is known into a reasoned position by arranging the information into a conceptual framework and a logical order.

Creating a conceptual framework. To learn, students must, first, form or be aware of concepts and, second, organize the concepts into a structure that relates them in some meaningful way. This process of conceptualizing promotes understanding of what is being studied and long-term retention of what is being learned.

First, students form concepts. A concept names a person, place, thing, or event that has certain characteristics. A golden retriever, for example, is a dog bred to hunt and retrieve birds, is friendly and loyal, motivated to please its owner, and motivated to use its terrific sense of smell. All this information helps define the concept "golden retriever." A concept pattern exists when all the information presented relates to a single word or phrase.

An important aspect of defining and understanding concepts is differentiating a concept from other concepts, identifying the similarity or dissimilarity between concepts. For example, two dogs can be seen as very similar: They both have four legs, they both have big teeth, they both wag their tails. But the same two dogs can be seen as very different: One is big and one is small, one is brown and one is black, one is fast and one is slow. Similarity and dissimilarity patterns exist when two or more concepts are compared and their similarities and dissimilarities noted.

Second, concepts must be organized into a structure that relates them in some meaningful way, into a rationale to support the assigned position. Four methods of doing so are an outline, a web network, a hierarchy, and a causal network. These methods of organizing concepts provide students with a means of summarizing and integrating important information.

To learn, students must, first, form or be aware of concepts and, second, organize the concepts into a structure that relates them in some meaningful way.

1. *Outline.* To build a coherent position out of isolated facts, students arrange the evidence into a sequence that makes sense to listeners by constructing an outline. Four types of outlines are simple, persuasive, AIDA, and PPF. A simple outline consists of a major idea followed by several supporting ideas. A more complex, persuasive outline is commonly divided into three parts: opening, body, and conclusion. The AIDA outline is designed to win listeners' **a**ttention, arouse their **i**nterest, create a **d**esire, and stimulate **a**ction or **a**greement. The PPF outline describes the **p**ast (there was a time when), **p**resent (but today, things have changed), and **f**uture (as we look ahead).
2. *Web network.* A web network (figure 4) is a wheel in which a main idea, important fact, or conclusion is in

the center, with supporting ideas and information radiating from it. The purpose of the web network is to clarify what students know about a concept. In the center of the wheel, for example, students may place the concept "Paul Revere." Radiating from the center the students then write down words that describe Paul Revere—patriot, American, man, revolutionary, silversmith, brave. Doing so helps clarify their concept of Paul Revere.

FIGURE 4

Web Networks

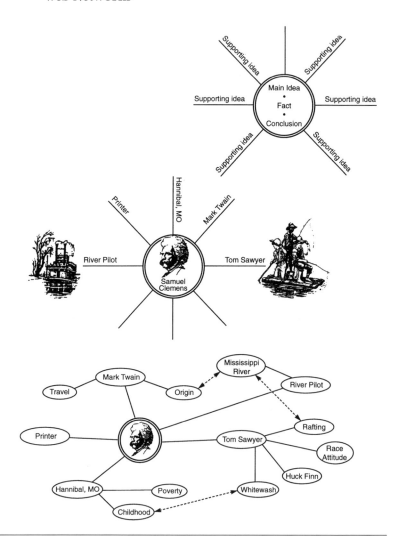

3. *Mind map.* A mind map is an expanded web network that has four major features: (1) a key idea in the center circle, (2) subideas in circles clustered around the center circle, (3) supporting ideas for each subidea in circles clustered around the appropriate circle, and (4) connectors that show relationships drawn from the key idea to the subideas, from the subideas to their supporting ideas, and from any supporting ideas that are related to each other or to other subideas. The purpose of a mind map is to help clarify the relationships among various ideas. Mind maps may be used for taking notes during a lecture or from a reading assignment, exploring new ideas, planning a course of action, or generating and organizing the ideas to be contained in a written essay or report.

4. *Venn diagrams.* Many times it is helpful to list how two ideas or things are similar and dissimilar. A comparison of golden retrievers and toy poodles, for example, shows the two breeds are similar in some ways and different in others. A Venn diagram (figure 5) consists of two or more overlapping circles that show what is similar and what is different about two (or more) concepts. To make a Venn diagram, draw two overlapping circles (each circle representing one concept), list the similar characteristics of the two concepts in the overlapping section, and, in the separate parts, list characteristics of the concept being described that are not true of the other concept.

5. *Hierarchy.* Information can be arranged into two types of hierarchies: part-to-whole hierarchies, in which the whole is broken down into parts, and class or category hierarchies, in which concepts are classified from the generic to the specific (figure 6).

6. *Causal networks.* A causal network organizes information in sequence so that one or more events are shown to have caused another. The message communicated is that if "a," "b," and "c" occur, then "d" will follow. For example, "If you stand at the highest point around and hold a metal golf club above your head during a thunderstorm, you will likely be struck by lighting."

For any issue, the relevant information must be assembled and organized into a pattern. Which information is selected to be used and presented depends on the pattern students use. Moreover, the importance of the information changes according to the pattern in which it is placed. Different patterns can be used to organize the same information, and some information may be important for one pattern but not for another.

FIGURE 5
Venn Diagram

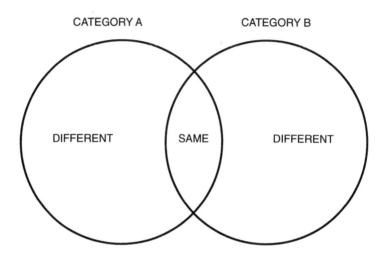

FIGURE 6
Hierarchies

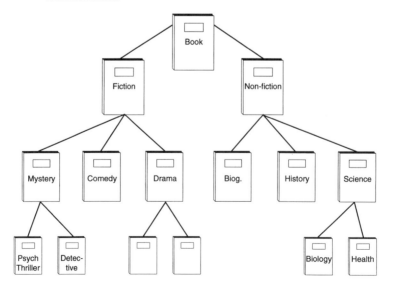

Creating a logical sequence. A logical sequence is created through the combined use of inductive and deductive logic (figure 7). Inductive and deductive logic go hand in hand. Inductive logic is used to establish general principles, deductive logic to apply a general principle to a specific case. Both are used to create a persuasive argument.

FIGURE 7

Logic

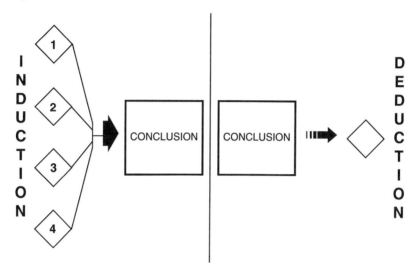

Inductive reasoning. "Has anything escaped me?" I asked with some self-importance. "I trust there is nothing of consequence that I have overlooked?"

"I'm afraid, my dear Watson, that most of your conclusions were erroneous. When I said that you stimulated me I meant, to be frank, that in noting your fallacies I was occasionally guided towards the truth" (Sir Arthur Conan Doyle, *The Hound of the Baskervilles*).

After an issue has been analyzed conceptually and all known information about the issue grouped into categories, it is placed into a logical structure involving both inductive and deductive reasoning. Induction is "leading into" (*in + ducere* = to lead) a conclusion, while deduction is "leading away from" a general conclusion to its particular parts and consequences.

In 1620, Sir Francis Bacon described inductive reasoning in his famous *Novum Organum, sive indicia vera de interpretatione naturae* ("The New Instrument, or true evidence concerning the interpretation of nature"). His new instrument changed the entire course of thought. Bacon believed that deductive reasoning was too rigid to measure nature's subtlety. He proposed that observed facts should create doubt about old ideas and that theories replace "truths."

Inductive reasoning involves taking known facts, information, experiences, and evidence and reaching a "likely" conclusion. It involves thinking through the evidence to a general conclusion. Making a decision, constructing a conclusion to summarize the known facts, or explaining something is engaging in inductive reasoning. All inductive conclusions are uncertain (not 100 percent certain). One plus some never equals all! There is never enough evidence for certitude. Inductive reasoning, therefore, results in tentative conclusions that are stated as probabilities, not certainties.

Deductive reasoning. While inductive reasoning goes from specific instances to a conclusion, deduction leads away from a general statement or conclusion to specific instances. Deductive reasoning can be defined as applying a generalization to specific instances. Deduction and induction move back and forth in much of our reasoning, complementing and supplementing each other. Inductive reasoning results in a conclusion or general statement based on a number of specific instances; deductive reasoning then takes that conclusion or general statement and applies it to additional specific instances.

Deductive reasoning is carried on in syllogisms, a word whose origins are from the Greek *syllogismos*, a combination of *syn*, meaning "together" and *logismos*, meaning "logical discourse." The word "synthesis," an intellectual bringing together of ideas and facts, also originates from *syllogismos*. A syllogism is a bringing together of two statements to arrive at a conclusion. Of the two statements, one is a generalization (the major premise), the second a specific factual statement (the minor premise) related to the general statement. A syllogism brings together two "knowns" into a new assertion (the conclusion). The general structure is as follows:

All A are B.
C is A.
Therefore, C is B.

Leaping to a conclusion

In an academic controversy, students are assigned a position and the tasks of preparing and presenting the best case possible for that position. In preparing the best case possible for the assigned position, students research the issue and organize the evidence into a conceptual framework and a logical sequence that leads the audience step by step to conclude that the position is valid and correct. Conclusions, however, are never completely proved, because we never know everything there is to know about a thesis or claim. Three parts are involved in reaching a conclusion: (1) what is known; (2) what is unknown or yet to be discovered; and (3) the conclusion that the thesis is valid and correct or invalid and incorrect.

To analyze information critically, students must be aware of what they do and do not know, the strength of the evidence on both sides of an issue, and the need to keep conclusions tentative so that they can derive an even more reasoned position in the future. A more reasoned position is derived by incorporating new information into conceptual frameworks and changing positions when the evidence indicates it is appropriate to do so.

Preparing to present your position

Quickly, bring me a beaker of wine so that I may wet my brain and say something clever.

—Aristophanes

Once the evidence has been gathered and organized into a compelling rationale, students must plan how to present their assigned position and its rationale with vigor, sincerity, and persuasiveness while keeping an open mind. In doing so, students must understand the audience's perspective, use more than one modality, and practice the presentation before delivering it for real.

Taking a perspective. "The first duty of a wise advocate is to convince his opponents that he understands their arguments and sympathizes with their just feelings" (Samuel Taylor Coleridge). For Pair A to persuade the proponents of the opposing position (Pair B) to accept their evidence and adopt their position, Pair A must speak from Pair B's perspective. Students should organize their presentation by putting themselves in the opponents' shoes. They need to analyze what it will take to motivate the members of the opposing pair to understand and agree with them and then develop their ideas to best supply that motivation.

Using more than one modality. Students should do more than just speak in presenting their position. Most often, visual displays are used to clarify, reinforce, or support points during a presentation. Visuals should be large enough so listeners can see them easily, be colorful, be simple and easily understood, and convey the meaning of the points being made.

Practicing. Students need to practice their presentation, preferably with the aid of someone who will give helpful feedback. After preparing their presentation, therefore, students meet with another pair who has the same position. Each pair practices its presentation, listens carefully to the other pair's presentations, and discusses how to improve each other's presentation. Each pair is to take something from the other presentation and use it to improve its own.

Required Social/Cognitive Skills

Several social and cognitive skills are needed to work with a partner to formulate a rationale for an assignment:

1. *Seek mastery* by summarizing out loud what has just been read, heard, or discussed as completely as possible without referring to notes or to the original material. Include all the important ideas and facts in the summary. Every member of the group must summarize often from memory both his own and the opposing position if learning is to be maximized.
2. *Seek accuracy* by correcting a member's summary, adding important information he or she did not include, and pointing out ideas or facts that were summarized incorrectly.
3. *Seek elaboration* by asking other members to relate the material being learned to earlier material and to other things they know.
4. *Seek clever ways* of remembering the important ideas

and facts by using drawings, mental pictures, and other memory aids.
5. *Make implicit reasoning overt* and thus open to correction and discussion by asking other group members to vocalize the reasoning they used to arrive at their conclusions.
6. *Plan how to teach* the material to others by asking other members to plan out loud how they would teach another student the material being studied. Planning how best to communicate the material can improve the quality of reasoning strategies and retention.
7. *Generate additional alternative answers* by going beyond the first answer or conclusion and producing a number of plausible answers to choose from.

Summary

The first step in structuring an academic controversy is presenting an issue that has both pro and con points of view, assigning students to a cooperative learning group of four members, dividing the group into two pairs, and assigning each pair one side of the issue. Pairs of students then prepare the best case possible for their assigned position. To do so, they must research the issue to collect all the evidence they can find to support their assigned position, organize the evidence into a conceptual framework that logically leads the audience to conclude that the position presented is valid and correct, leap to the conclusion that their assigned position is valid, and present the position and its rationale to the opposing pair. Students now have a plan for presenting that position with vigor, sincerity, and persuasiveness while keeping an open mind.

ADVOCATING A POSITION

*. . . instead of looking on discussion as a stumbling
block in the way of action, we think it an indispensable
preliminary to any wise action at all.*

—Pericles

We live in a society that highly values the notion that truth is
more likely to be approximated if opposing views can be
freely and openly expressed. Rooted in the ancient Athenian
tradition of a democratic, open society, we encourage rather
than suppress the expression of opposing views. We labor
in the faith that truth will spring from the uninhibited clash
of opposing views. Such clashes begin with researching a
topic, organizing and conceptualizing the evidence, taking
the leap to a conclusion, and then advocating that conclusion to the best of one's ability. Advocacy is the presentation
of a position, providing reasons why others should adopt it.
Advocacy is essential for ensuring that the assigned position
receives a complete and fair hearing and for teaching the
opposing students the information one is presenting (see
table 6). In advocating their assigned positions, students:

1. Keep in mind that the overall goal is for the group to
   make a reasoned judgment about the issue. Members of
   the group must therefore learn the evidence and reasoning contained in both sides of the issue to create an
   insightful and illuminating synthesis or integration.
2. Present and advocate the position with the intent of
   persuading the other group members of its validity,
   ensuring that it gets a fair and complete hearing, and
   teaching the information to the opposing students.
3. Learn the opposing position and perspective to better
   understand and refute it.
4. Refute the evidence supporting the opposing position
   and the reasoning used to organize that evidence.
   Critical analysis subjects each position to a trial by fire in
   which the opposition challenges the strength of the
   evidence and the validity of the reasoning.
5. Rebut the opposition's attacks on the validity of the
   evidence and reasoning contained in their own position.
6. Search for further evidence and a better conceptualization.
7. Use social and cognitive skills for challenging the other
   position and defending their own.

TABLE 6

Advocating Your Position

Advocates of Position A	Advocates of Position B
Present Position A persuasively	Present Position B persuasively
Learn Position B	Learn Position A
Refute Position B	Refute Position A
Rebut attacks on Position A	Rebut attacks on Position B
Search for new information and reconsider	Search for new information and reconsider
Adopt a revised tentative conclusion	Adopt a revised tentative conclusion

Presenting Your Position

I take it we are all in complete agreement on the decision here. . . . Then I propose we postpone further discussion until our next meeting to give ourselves time to develop disagreement and perhaps gain some understanding of what the decision is all about.
— Alfred Sloan, former chair of General Motors

During a controversy, participants present and advocate positions to others who, in turn, advocate opposing positions. In essence, students' responsibility is to say, "Here is the best case for my assigned position. I am going to ensure that it receives a fair hearing and full consideration." The format for presenting a position contains two steps:

1. Person A presents his or her position as sincerely and thoroughly as he or she can. Person B listens carefully and takes notes.
2. The students reverse presenting/listening roles.

The guidelines for making a persuasive presentation are as follows:

1. The presentation should begin with a thesis statement or claim and a strong, sincere, and enthusiastic appeal for the listeners' agreement with the thesis or claim. Both the position being taken and the presenters' conviction and enthusiasm should be clear.
2. The rationale for the thesis or claim should be presented. It should consist of a conceptual framework

containing several points of evidence arranged in a logical sequence. Evidence to support the validity of the thesis or claim should be presented in a well-conceptualized framework. To ensure that the audience does not miss the important points, each major point included in the rationale should be clearly stated, stated again in different words, illustrated with an example, story, anecdote, or visual display, and stated once more.

3. The presentation should end with a conclusion that is the same as the thesis or claim and a strong note of appeal.

4. The presentation should be delivered with enthusiasm, conviction, and sincerity. It should be an appeal, a call for action to consider the viewpoint. Unless the presenter has convictions and can illustrate them in a well-conceptualized and logical form, the presenter has nothing to say. The first sentence should wake opponents up and make them listen. The conclusion should wind up on a strong note of appeal. The presenter has to convince the audience to listen and to consider the position with open minds.

5. The presenters should not try to cover too much in their initial presentations and save some of their evidence for the open discussion. During the initial presentation, it may be best for students to select a few major points (four or five at the most) and expand on them by use of examples, illustrations, stories, and anecdotes.

6. The presenters should make eye contact with opponents. They should first look directly at one person for a few seconds, then look at the other so no one feels left out of the presentation.

7. The presentation should be conducted within the time limits stated.

8. The presentation should use more than one medium. Visual aids help students present their positions convincingly and clearly.

9. Students should practice their presentation until they are comfortable delivering it and can do so naturally. Practice makes perfect.

It is important to present the best evidence available, organized into well-conceptualized and logically valid frameworks.

Learning Opposing Positions and Perspectives

. . . it is critical that one seek to understand [other peoples'] perceptions if one is to understand the circumstances under which their behavior might change.
—Harold J. Leavitt, organizational psychologist

Two primary purposes of the controversy procedure are for students to teach what they know to their opponents and to learn the opposing evidence and perspective. The opposition's position and perspective must be thoroughly understood to create a synthesis based on the best reasoning by both sides, to be able to refute the opposing position, and to do well on a test covering both sides of the issue. Learning the opposing information and perspective (position) is facilitated by:

1. Listening carefully to the opposing presentation.
2. Asking for additional evidence, facts, and information.
3. Clarifying anything that is not understood by paraphrasing it.
4. Taking notes detailing the information and evidence being presented.
5. Drawing a picture of the information and evidence being presented.
6. Thinking of other supporting evidence that the opposing students did not present but that would strengthen their position.

Open Discussion of the Issue

When two men in business always agree, one of them is unnecessary.
—William Wrigley, Jr.

Once the issue is researched and the positions presented, an open, free-for-all discussion takes place. The goals of the discussion are to ensure that all group members understand both sides of the issue thoroughly and completely, to allow students to continue to advocate the best case for their assigned position, to subject each position to a trial by fire in which the opposition critically analyzes and challenges the strength of the evidence and the validity of the reasoning, to allow students the chance to defend their assigned position and rebut the attacks being made on it, and to allow the uncertainty created by the critical analyses and challenges to motivate a search for additional information and a reconceptualization of the issue. The procedure is as follows:

1. Students present arguments forcefully and persuasively, emphasizing evidence and reasoning.
2. Students listen critically to the opposing position, trying to find flaws in evidence and reasoning. They ask for facts and rationale to clarify their understanding.
3. Students attack the opposing position, pointing out the weaknesses, flaws, and mistakes in the evidence and reasoning.
4. Students defend their position from the opponents' attacks, presenting counterarguments, clarification, and extensions.

Students prepare themselves to make a reasoned judgment by ensuring that each position gets a fair and complete hearing . . . and a critical examination.

Students should keep in mind that the overall goal is to make a reasoned judgment about the issue, and they therefore must learn the evidence and reasoning contained in the opposing position. Reasoned judgment requires a thorough understanding of all sides of the issue. Students prepare themselves to make a reasoned judgment by ensuring that each position gets a fair and complete hearing (through having classmates advocate it strongly) and a critical examination (through having classmates attempt to refute it).

Continuing advocacy
During the open discussion, students are responsible for the continued advocacy of their assigned position to ensure that it gets a complete and fair hearing and that opposing students learn the information presented. In continuing to advocate their position, students present arguments forcefully and persuasively, emphasizing facts and evidence. The more persistently, consistently, and confidently they present their positions, the more credible the positions are perceived to be (Nemeth, Swedlund, and Kanki 1974; Nemeth and Wachtler 1983). Moreover, advocacy tends to increase learning. The process of argument and counterargument aimed at persuading others to adopt, modify, or drop positions requires students to contribute information, repeat information, elaborate on the material being discussed, critically evaluate the

validity and correctness of claims, critically evaluate evidence, and use higher-level reasoning processes.

Refuting the opposing position

> *. . . the noise could be heard all over the city. Our fights over words were furious, blasphemous, and frequent, but even in their hottest moments we both knew that we were arguing academically and not personally.*
>
> —Richard Rogers,
> recalling his work with Larry Hart

Refutation means to attack another person's position in an attempt to weaken or even destroy it. Refutation is an attempt to cast significant doubt on and/or show the inadequacies of the opposition's evidence and reasoning so that they (or interested other people) will be willing to change their minds. Charging the opposition with having faulty evidence or using faulty reasoning is a standard practice in refutation.

Refuting the opponent's evidence. Imagine that your students are involved in a controversy over Shakespeare's *Hamlet*. Two students in each cooperative group advocate the position that Hamlet was indecisive. Two students advocate the position that Hamlet was very decisive but had bad luck, never catching his stepfather at the right moment. One pair might say, "Hamlet was indecisive. Trust us on this one. We are right." The other pair asks for evidence: "We know your opinion; where are your facts? Show us the passages in the play that support your thesis."

In a controversy, students do not blindly believe each other's opinions. They differentiate between fact and opinion. A fact is a thing, state, or event that can be verified by the senses (measuring, weighing, counting) or by making an inference from physical data so strong as to allow no other explanation. An opinion is an unproven belief or judgment. "Columbus reached American in 1492" is a fact. "Columbus was a great man" is an opinion. If students are not sure whether a statement is a fact or an opinion, they should treat it as an opinion.

In a controversy, students also ask for evidence, which they critically examine to determine whether it is valid or faulty. Evidence can be faulty for a number of reasons. The procedure for evaluating evidence is as follows:

1. *Determine whether the claim can be supported by evidence.* A supportable claim can be supported by evidence in the form it is stated. Claims that cannot be supported by evidence in the form they are stated require clarification. For example, *vague claims* are impossible to support because they convey no distinct meaning (their interpretation is too open)—"This house is a pig pen!" "Teachers are lazy!" Such statements are open to many interpretations and are therefore too vague to support. *Ambiguous claims* can be interpreted in two or more very different ways—"The shooting of the police was justifiable" (did the police shoot or were they shot?). *Meaningless claims* use contrived terms intended to promote a false impression—"Our product is new and improved" or "This is light butter." *Euphemisms* substitute a mild expression for a blunt one to soften the meaning of certain information or employ vague words that cannot be supported as claims—"The cat had an accident" or "The horse should be put to sleep."

2. *Determine whether there is enough evidence to validate the claim.* The evidence presented may be of insufficient quantity if there is not enough of it or only some of it is presented (that is, key evidence is omitted).

3. *Determine whether the evidence presented is of sufficient quality.* Evidence lacks quality when it is inaccurate, outdated, biased, or irrelevant to the claim. Evidence also lacks quality if the presenter is not qualified to make the judgments being presented.

4. *Determine whether the evidence is reliable.* The evidence is unreliable if the presenter *oversimplifies causal relationships* by presenting information that is partially true while excluding a great deal of necessary other information. Ignoring the complexity and number of causes for an event distorts reality. For example, to say that the cause of the Civil War was slavery in the southern states is not totally incorrect, but it oversimplifies the reasons for the war. Such errors are common, and students should be able to recognize them. The evidence also is unreliable if it *lacks a credible source* (originates from a source of

insufficient credibility), *slants the information* (is based on slanted or biased information), or *appeals to emotion* (its intent is to stir up emotions rather than inform).

If the claim can be supported by evidence that is of sufficient quantity, quality, and reliability, then the claim is substantiated.

Refuting the opponent's reasoning. "Our advantage," noted Francis Crick, Nobel Prize winner and codiscoverer of the double helix:

> *was that we had evolved unstated but fruitful methods of collaboration. . . . If either of us suggested a new idea, the other, while taking it seriously, would attempt to demolish it in a candid but nonhostile manner.*

Not only can the evidence presented to support a position be faulty, but the reasoning used to organize the evidence can also be faulty. The procedure for evaluating reasoning is as follows:

1. *Determine whether there are errors of perception based on a limited or inadequate perspective.* Errors of perception are faulty ways of seeing reality, preventing persons from being open-minded even before they begin to think. Some common errors of perception are a "mine is better" competitive orientation; selective perception, including perceiving evidence that supports current ideas and rejecting anything that challenges them; pretensions of knowing; resistance to change; and either/or dualistic thinking, that is, taking extreme positions on an issue when other positions are possible.
2. *Determine whether there are errors of judgment*—flaws in reasoning that occur in the process of sorting out and assessing evidence. Some common errors of judgment are overgeneralizing, making unwarranted assumptions, and failing to make distinctions. Overgeneralizing involves reaching conclusions that far exceed the available evidence, such as "Nothing can be worse than losing the championship game" or "Everyone from Edina is a rich snob." Faulty generalizations can also result from the opposition's being too hasty, using an insufficient num-

ber of instances, using the wrong qualifier, exaggerating the evidence, using untypical or biased instances, and not considering plausible alternative explanations. One important type of overgeneralizing is the use of stereotypes that prevent students from seeing important differences among individual people, places, and things.

Assumptions are ideas taken for granted. They are usually implied rather than expressed and are therefore often hard to detect. *Unwarranted assumptions* occur when a person takes too much for granted and therefore does not ask useful questions and explore possibilities. Students should consider what the presenter has taken for granted and decide whether it is warranted or not.

Distinctions are subtle differences among things. Care in making distinctions helps individuals overcome confusion and deal with complex issues effectively. Important distinctions are between a person and an idea (judge an idea on its own merits, not on who presented it), between an assertion and the evidence (judge ideas on how well supported—and supportable—they are), between familiarity and validity (hearing an assertion often does not make it true), and "always" and "often" or "never" and "seldom."

3. *Determine whether there are errors of reaction.* Errors of reaction are defensive ways to preserve a self-image. They occur when one person expresses a position and another person reacts negatively. Some common errors of reaction are explaining away, shifting the burden of proof, and attacking the presenter. If, for example, students explain away challenges to their ideas, they will not succeed in altering reality; they will only postpone dealing with it. And the longer the postponement, the more painful the experience. It is better to face unpleasant ideas directly and honestly.

Accepting the burden of proof means supporting one's assertions with evidence, with the burden of proof falling on the person who makes the assertion. The more the assertions challenge accepted wisdom, the greater the burden of proof. If students make an assertion and find they cannot defend it, they should not shift the burden of proof to the challenger. Instead, they should withdraw the assertion. Further, when the message is unpleasant or disturbing, they should resist the tendency to attack the messenger.

4. *Determine whether there are errors in the way ideas are interrelated.* A person listening to persuasive arguments should listen for certain key words, which tell the listener what type of relationship among ideas is being presented. *And relationships* (signaled by "also," "in addition," "next," "further," "moreover," "besides," "another," "finally") may signal that more evidence is being offered to support an assertion and that what follows adds to what preceded. *But relationships* (signaled by "however," "nevertheless," "yet," "in contrast") signal that what follows contrasts with what preceded and may signal that an exception or qualification is to follow. *Therefore relationships* (signaled by "so," "consequently," "accordingly," "thus," "it follows that") signal that a conclusion is being made about the preceding evidence.
5. *Determine whether there are errors of logic,* which occur when students use faulty inductive or deductive reasoning, such as asserting the consequent or denying the antecedent.

Rebutting attacks on one's own position

When the opposition points out faulty evidence and reasoning, students can give up and agree with the opposing pair or they can defend their position and its rationale. In defending their position from the opponents' attacks, students present counterarguments, clarifications, and extensions, thereby rebutting the attacks on their position. Rebuttal, or resubstantiation, is the rebuilding of one's case that has been attacked by the opponent. Students clarify their evidence and reasoning and present further evidence. The fire of the refutation tempers and strengthens students' rationales and understanding of the issue being studied. It also creates uncertainty, conceptual conflict, and disequilibrium. In structured academic controversies, refutation and rebuttal are constants.

Students should summarize the opposing position frequently and concisely for at least three reasons. First, a summary is an excellent way for students to increase their understanding of the opposing position. Second, a summary helps illuminate the inadequacies of the opposing position by reviewing how evidence and reasoning have been unraveled and refuted. Third, a summary clarifies what students agree and disagree on and what is "true" and "untrue." Complex positions can be broken down into subissues and a spreadsheet constructed to help analyze the validity of the evidence and reasoning for each subissue. An effective summary is expressed in the student's own words, emphasizes the key points, and is accurate.

Caucus with the Practice Partner

In the middle of the open discussion, students may caucus with their partner and compare notes on how they think they are doing. Students should discuss the arguments the other side has advanced and plan how to refute them, and discuss the attacks the other side is making on their position and plan how to rebut them.

Searching for Further Evidence and A Better Conceptualization

The more the opposition challenges students' evidence and reasoning, unravels students' arguments, and points out students' errors of perception, judgment, and reaction, the more uncertain students become. Conceptual conflict, uncertainty, and disequilibrium tend to result when students hear other alternatives being advocated, have their position criticized and refuted, and are challenged by information that is incompatible with and does not fit with their conclusions. Uncertainty tends to motivate an active search for more information in the hope of resolving the conceptual conflict. Indices of epistemic curiosity include individuals' actively searching for more information, seeking to understand opposing positions and rationales, and attempting to view the situation from numerous perspectives. The uncertainty is heightened by the students' knowing that they have to learn (and pass a test on) the information being presented by the opposing pair. The more uncertain students become, the more they should be encouraged to seek out further information about the issue and use the new information in reconceptualizing the rationale for their position.

Using Social and Cognitive Skills for Challenging And Defending a Position

Several social and cognitive skills are involved in challenging opponents' conclusions and evidence and defending one's own position from attack:

1. *Group members should be critical of ideas, not of individuals.* Arguments should concern ideas, not personality traits, and there should be nothing personal in disagreements. Members should be highly critical of each other's ideas while affirming each other's competence. They should look each other in the eye and say, "I can see why you think that from your perspective, but I see it differently." Or "I have great respect for your intelligence and I am therefore taking what you say very seriously, but right now I have a different opinion." When disagreeing with another person, students should criticize his or her ideas and conclusions while communicating respect and appreciation for him or her as a person. Any implication of incompetence or weakness and any hint of rejecting another member should be avoided. The focus is on the position and its rationale, not on the person. Defensiveness should not be provoked through attacks on the person. "I appreciate you and I am interested in your ideas, but I disagree with your current position" should be communicated rather than "You are stupid and ignorant."

2. *Group members should not take personally other members' disagreements with and rejection of their ideas.* Students should take disagreement with their ideas and conclusions as an interesting opportunity to learn something new, not as a personal attack, rejection, or disrespect. Students should always separate the quality of their rationale from their competence and worth as a person.

3. *Group members should remember that the ultimate goal is to formulate a joint position everyone agrees with.* The controversy is to take place within a cooperative learning group. A group report is required at the end of the unit, and every group member will take a test covering all sides of the issue being studied. While the immediate task is to evaluate critically and challenge the opposing position and its rationale, the long-term goal is to ensure that members learn the opposing rationale and teach their evidence to the opposing pair.

4. *Members should ensure that there are several cycles of differentiation (bringing out differences in positions) and integration (combining several positions into one new, creative position) before a final consensus is reached.* Differentiation must come before integration is

attempted. Specifically, *differentiation* involves seeking out and clarifying differences among members' ideas, information, conclusions, theories, and opinions. It involves highlighting the differences among members' reasoning and seeking to understand fully what the different positions and perspectives are. All different points of view must be presented and explored thoroughly before new, creative solutions are sought. *Integration/ synthesis* involves combining group members' information, reasoning, theories, and conclusions into a single position that satisfies them all. After it has differentiated positions, the group must seek a new, creative position that synthesizes the thinking of all members. Group members should never try to integrate different positions before adequate differentiation has taken place. The potential for integration is never greater than the adequacy of the differentiation already achieved. Most controversies go through a series of differentiations and integrations before a final consensus is reached.

5. *An important aspect of differentiation is asking for justification why the member's conclusion or answer is the correct or appropriate one.* Students should ask, "Why do you think that way?" "What is the evidence that supports your position?" "Prove to me that what you are saying is correct." Students should clarify and seek others' rationale by questioning. They should probe by asking questions that lead to deeper understanding or analysis, such as "Would it work in this situation . . . ?" or "What else makes you believe . . . ?"

6. *Group members should try to refute each other's evidence or reasoning.* To do so requires conceptually taking the opposing rationale apart to determine whether the evidence or the reasoning is faulty.

7. *Group members should change their minds when they are logically persuaded to do so.* All conclusions are tentative, based on current evidence. As students learn more about the issue, they should change their minds (as long as they have subjected the new evidence to the fire of critical analysis).

Summary

After researching their position and constructing a convincing rationale, students are ready to advocate their assigned positions. Each side presents its position and supporting rationale. An open discussion follows. During the discussion, students critically analyze the opposing position and point out its shortcomings while defending their own position from the attacks of the opposing pair. Presenting a position includes advocacy and listening carefully to the opposing position. Refuting the opposing position and rebutting attacks on one's own position includes advocacy, learning the opposing position, critically analyzing the evidence used by the opposition (so its weaknesses, flaws, and mistakes can be revealed), critically analyzing the logic used by the opposition, reducing uncertainty by seeking further information and reconceptualizing the issue, and using the necessary social and cognitive skills.

WHICH BOOKS DO WE TAKE?

Tasks: During this semester, you have read a number of books for this literature class. From the list of all the assigned books, choose three that you would save if the Earth were going to be destroyed, and write a report detailing your rationale for saving these three books over the others. In doing so, make sure all group members are prepared to take the test on the books read this semester.

Scientists have suddenly discovered a large comet headed toward Earth. All life, if not Earth itself, will be destroyed. Your group of four members has been picked to move from Earth to a new planet, where the conditions will be harsh and difficult. You will be starting life over, trying to develop a farming and technological society at the same time. Because of limited room in the spaceship, you can bring only three books. "Think carefully," the captain says. "You will never return to Earth, and you will never be able to get more books from Earth."

Cooperative: Write one report for the group of four. All members must agree. Everyone has to be able to explain the choices made and the reasons they are good ones.

Procedure:

1. *Research and prepare your position.* Your group of four has been divided into two pairs. Each pair is to make a list of three books to take and plan how to present the best case possible for its choices to the other pair.

2. *Present and advocate your position.* Forcefully and persuasively present the best case for your list to the opposing pair. Be as convincing

---

as possible. Take notes and clarify anything you do not understand when the opposing pair presents its position.

3. *Open discussion (advocate, refute, rebut).* Argue forcefully and persuasively for your list. Critically evaluate and challenge the opposing pair's list and reasoning and defend your reasoning from attack.

4. *Reverse perspectives.* Reverse perspectives and present the best case for the opposing list. The opposing pair will do the same. Strive to see the issue from both perspectives simultaneously.

5. *Synthesize.* Drop all advocacy. Synthesize and integrate the best evidence and reasoning from both sides into a joint list that all members can agree to. Then finalize the group report, present your conclusions to the class, ensure that all group members are prepared to take the test, and process how well you worked together as a group and how you could be even more effective next time.

MAKING THE DECISION

The test of a first-rate intelligence is the ability to hold two opposed ideas in the mind at the same time, and still retain the ability to function.

— F. Scott Fitzgerald

Reversing Perspectives

The position has been researched and a persuasive argument prepared, presented, and advocated. Students have critically evaluated the opposing position, unraveled it, examined it for faulty evidence and reasoning, and checked it for reasoning errors. In doing so, students have learned the information contained in the opposing pair's arguments. To complete the sequence, students must step back and see the issue from both perspectives simultaneously. To help students move beyond the perspective of their assigned position, they are required to present the opposing position (the rationale and perspective) to the opposing students' satisfaction. Group members can then drop all advocacy and reach a consensus on the issue. At that point, students complete a group report and then individually take a test on both sides of the issue.

In a controversy, students are asked to adopt a specific perspective that is different from the perspectives of others. A *perspective* is a way of viewing the world and one's relationship to it. *Perspective taking* is the ability to understand how a situation appears to another person and how that person reacts cognitively and emotionally to the situation. More specifically, a *cognitive perspective* consists of the cognitive organization being used to give meaning to a person's knowledge and the structure of a person's reasoning. The opposite of perspective taking is *egocentrism,* or being unaware that other perspectives exist and that one's own view of the issue is incomplete and limited. Different people have different perspectives. Each person may have different perspectives at different times. Any issue being studied always has a variety of perspectives from which it can be viewed.

Understanding one's assigned perspective is not enough to create a thoughtful and insightful synthesis. To create a wise synthesis, students must have a clear understanding of all sides of the issue, an accurate assessment of their validity and relative merits, and the ability to think creatively to integrate the best reasoning from both sides and come up with potential syntheses. In other words, comprehending the information opponents present is not enough. Students must also clearly understand the cognitive perspective opponents are using to organize and interpret the information. Creating a synthesis is then based on students' seeing the issue from both their own and the opposing perspective and keeping both perspectives in mind at the same time.

To free students from their assigned perspective and to increase their understanding of the opposing perspective, students engage in *perspective reversal*—taking the opposing pair's position and sincerely and completely presenting the opposing position as if it were their own. The procedure for taking each other's perspectives in a controversy is as follows:

1. *Person A presents Person B's position.* Students are to present the opposing position as if it were theirs. They are to be forceful and persuasive, adding new arguments, facts, and rationale when it is possible. Everything the students did to present a convincing case for their original position should be done during perspective reversal to ensure that students can in fact see the issue from the opposing perspective. Person B corrects errors in Person A's presentation and notes omissions.
2. *Person B presents Person A's position.* Person A corrects errors in Person B's presentation and notes omissions.

An important issue for synthesizing is to keep both one's own and the other person's perspective in mind simultaneously. Such perspective taking is absolutely essential in controversy situations for a number of reasons (see D. Johnson [1971a] and D. Johnson and R. Johnson [1989] for a complete review of the research).

First, perspective taking improves communication and reduces misunderstandings and distortions by influencing how messages are phrased and received. Misunderstandings often occur because people assume that everyone sees the world through their perspective. The better one understands the other person's perspective, the more able he or she is to phrase messages so the other person can easily understand them. If a person does not know what snow is, for example, you do not refer to "corn snow" or "fresh powder." In addition, understanding the other person's perspective helps you accurately understand the messages you are receiving from that person. If the other person says, for example, "That's just great!" the meaning reverses if you know the person is frustrated. You must be able to stand in the sender's shoes to understand accurately the meaning of the messages that person is sending you. Engaging in perspective taking in controversy situations tends to increase understanding and retention of the opponent's information and perspective, facilitate the achievement of creative, high-quality problem solving, and promote more positive perceptions of the process of exchanging information, fellow group members, and the group's work (Falk and D. Johnson 1977; D. Johnson 1971a, 1977).

Second, perspective taking is essential for a realistic assessment of the validity of evidence and reasoning. To propose workable syntheses, one must understand how the other person sees the problem.

Third, the more able a student is to take the other person's perspective, the broader the picture he or she gets of the issue. Out of a mass of detailed information, people tend to pick out and focus on those facts that confirm their prior perceptions and to disregard or misinterpret those that call their perceptions into question. Each side tends to see only the merits of its own case and only the faults of the other side. It is not enough to logically understand how the other person views the problem. If you want to influence the other person, you also need to understand empathetically the power of his or her point of view and to feel the emotional force with which he or she believes in it.

Fourth, engaging in perspective taking tends to improve the relationship with the other person. You are more liked and respected when the other person realizes that you are seeing his or her perspective accurately and using it to create potential agreements that benefit both sides equally.

To free students from their assigned perspective and to increase their understanding of the opposing perspective, students engage in perspective reversal— taking the opposing pair's position . . .

Synthesizing and Integrating

The need to be right is a sign of a vulgar mind.
—Albert Camus

Controversies are resolved constructively when students create a synthesis based on the best evidence and reasoning from both sides of the issue. The procedure for this final stage of the controversy process involves six steps:

1. Drop all advocacy.
2. Summarize and synthesize the best evidence and rea-

soning from all sides of the issue into a joint position that all members can agree to.

3. Write a joint report based on a group consensus supported by evidence that explains the group's synthesis.
4. Present the group's conclusions to the class.
5. Individually take the test covering both sides of the issue.
6. Process how well members worked together as a group and how they could be even more effective next time.

Drop all advocacy

In the final step of structured academic controversy, students are to drop all advocacy, step back to achieve some objectivity, and try to view the issue from a variety of perspectives simultaneously. Students should strive to see new patterns within a body of evidence and generate a number of optional ways of integrating the evidence. By creating a number of operational syntheses, students help each other go beyond the original positions advocated and the first reasonable synthesis suggested. The more alternatives suggested, the less group members will be "frozen" to their original positions. Students unfreeze other members' fixation on their position by suggesting alternatives. The alternatives are then considered on their merits. Sometimes a member may be assigned the role of "generator" to ensure that additional positions are formulated. In generating possible syntheses, students may wish to follow the DOVE procedure: Defer judgment (any idea should be stated); opt for original, different ideas; use vast numbers of ideas; expand the list by piggybacking on other members' ideas.

Synthesize

We must learn to explore all the options and possibilities that confront us in a complex and rapidly changing world. We must learn to welcome and not fear the voices of dissent.

—J.W. Fulbright

Students are to summarize and synthesize the best arguments and evidence from other sides into a joint position that all group members can agree to. Synthesis occurs when students create a new position that subsumes the previous two. Often, for example, the process results in a thesis, a counterthesis, and then a synthesis that combines both. A synthesis is a new position that unifies the previous ones, brings them into harmony, and unites their best features at a higher level. The previous positions are seen as parts to be combined into a whole. Synthesis requires students to see new patterns within a body of evidence, view the issue from a variety of perspectives, and generate a number of optional alternative positions that subsume the evidence supporting the original two. In trying to create a synthesis, it is sometimes helpful to summarize the two original positions into a few words. Organizing large blocks of information into an abbreviated form often clarifies the underlying nature of the positions and illuminates the relationships and patterns in the evidence gathered by both sides, helping to synthesize the two positions.

Write a report
Students are expected to write a report, based on a group consensus supported by evidence, that explains the group's synthesis. The report should include:

1. A title page.
2. An introduction and statement of the issue.
3. The group's synthesis or new position.
4. The supporting evidence, organized to lead the reader step by step to a conclusion. Diagrams, pictures, and charts should be included to help the reader understand the paper and make it more interesting.
5. A conclusion that is the same as the group's synthesis.
6. A list of the references from which the evidence was gathered.

Neatness and style count. All of the material on planning a position is relevant to writing the final report.

Present the conclusions to the class
Each group must be ready to present its conclusions to the whole class, following the guidelines for making a good presentation in "Preparing a Position."

Individually take the test
Each student individually takes a test covering both sides of the issue. The group receives bonus points if all members score above a predetermined criterion of excellence.

Process how well the group did

The final step is for each group to process how well members worked together and how they could be even more effective next time. Celebrate the group's success (see "Using Academic Controversy").

Summary

In a controversy, students are asked to adopt a specific perspective (a way of viewing the world and his or her relationship to it) in preparing the best case for a position on an issue being studied. Adopting the assigned perspective is necessary to make sure that the position being represented receives a fair and complete hearing. To increase their understanding of the opposing perspective, students engage in a perspective reversal. Each pair presents the best case for the opposing position, being as sincere and enthusiastic as if the position were their own. Doing so has many benefits, including increasing students' ability to synthesize the best evidence and reasoning from both sides. Synthesizing occurs when students integrate a number of different ideas and facts into a single position. The dual purposes of synthesis are to arrive at the best possible position on the issue and to find a position that all group members can agree to and commit themselves to. In achieving these purposes, students should avoid the dualistic trap of choosing which position is "right" and which is "wrong," avoid the relativistic trap of stating that both positions are correct, depending on your perspective, and think probabilistically in formulating a synthesis that everyone can agree to.

SUMMING UP

The Necessity for Controversy

When controversy is suppressed and concurrence seeking emphasized, several defects in making decisions will appear. When NASA, for example, decided to launch the space shuttle *Challenger,* engineers at the Morton Thiokol Company (which makes the shuttle's rocket boosters) and at Rockwell International (which manufactures the orbiter) had opposed the launch because of dangers posed by the subfreezing temperatures. The Thiokol engineers feared that the cold would make the rubber seals at the joints between the rocket's four main segments too brittle to contain the rocket's superhot gases. Several months before the doomed mission, the company's top expert had warned in a memo that it was a "jump ball" as to whether the seal would hold and that if it failed, "the result would be a catastrophe of the highest order" (Magnuson 1986). In a group discussion the night before the launch, the engineers argued for a delay with their uncertain managers and the NASA officials who wanted to launch on schedule. Because the engineers could not prove the danger, they were silenced. Pressures to conform were aimed at the engineers, such as a NASA official's complaint, "My God, Thiokol, when do you want me to launch, next April?" NASA managers made a pact with the Thiokol managers to shut the engineers out of the decision making. Finally, the top NASA executive who made the final decision to launch was never told about the engineers' concerns or about Rockwell officials' reservations. Protected from the disagreeable information, he confidently gave the go-ahead to launch *Challenger* on its tragic flight.

How could such faulty decision making take place? The answer is because of the lack of controversy. NASA officials never gave the alternative of delaying the launch a fair and complete hearing. Disagreement was stifled rather than used. Often in group discussions if a margin of support for one alternative develops, then better ideas have little chance of being accepted. In mob lynchings, for example, misgivings, if not immediately expressed, were drowned out. Drawing on biased information is evident in some group polarization experiments; often the arguments that surfaced in group discussion tended to be more one-sided than those volunteered privately by individuals. Group discussions can exacerbate tendencies toward overconfidence, thereby heightening an illusion of judgmental accuracy (Dunning and Ross 1988). Minority opinions can be suppressed. When initially only one member of a six-member group knew the correct answer, the single member failed to convince the others almost 75 percent of the time because he or she was not given a fair and complete hearing (Laughlin 1980; Laughlin and Adamopoulos 1980). Group decision making often goes wrong because alternatives are not considered carefully, minority opinions are silenced, and disagreement among members' conclusions is suppressed.

What is true in decision making is also true for learning situations. Stifling disagreement, seeking support for only one alternative view, drawing on biased information, suppressing information to make arguments one-sided, creating an illusion of judgmental accuracy, becoming overconfident, not considering alternative viewpoints, silencing minority opinions, and suppressing disagreement all destroy the discovery of knowledge and "truth." Students learn how to engage in constructive intellectual conflicts by using academic controversies. When using controversies in the classroom, however, faculty need to understand:

1. The lure of suppressing intellectual conflict.
2. The dangers of controversy.
3. What is and what is not an academic controversy.
4. How to respond when unanticipated controversies arise in the classroom.
5. The importance of academic controversy for teaching students how to be contributing citizens in a democracy.

The lure of suppressing intellectual disagreement
Educators seem drawn to suppressing intellectual conflict in the classroom. Students are told not to talk to each other. All communication is to be directed to the instructor in response to direct questions. Students generally are expected not to intellectually challenge the instructor or each other. Much of the traditional teaching method of lecture, class discussion, and individual worksheets eliminates most possibilities for intellectual disagreement and academic controversy. Instructors are generally anxious about the possibility of poorly managed conflicts in the classroom; they generally have received no training in the procedures to use conflict for academic reasons. The diversity of students in most classrooms results in students' having markedly different ideas about how intellectual conflicts should be managed.

Instructors generally do not teach their students the procedures and skills they need to engage in constructive arguments. Conflicts, moreover, are often complex and take time to resolve. For these and many other reasons, academic conflicts are suppressed and avoided in most classrooms.

The dangers of controversy

While the many advantages of controversy are apparent, it can be dangerous to engage students in a controversy under certain conditions. When the overall classroom climate is competitive, asking students to disagree and argue with each other can result in hurt feelings, anger, resentment, close-minded rejection of other points of view, and damage to relationships. When viewpoints and information are not heterogeneous enough, controversy does not occur and the process is trivialized. When students are unskilled and behave in hostile and antagonistic ways, controversy can have many destructive outcomes. And if students are unable to reason logically and rationally, the procedure will be a waste of time.

What academic controversy is not

Conducting an academic controversy and dealing with controversial issues and controversial subjects in the classroom are often misunderstood. A *controversial issue* is an issue for which society has not found consensus; it is considered so significant that each proposed way of dealing with the issue has ardent supporters and adamant opponents. Controversial issues, by nature, arouse protest from some individuals or groups, as any position taken will be opposed by those who favor another position. The protest may result from a feeling that a cherished belief, an economic interest, or a basic principle is threatened. Academic controversy is aimed at learning, not at resolving political issues in a community.

In many places, parents are concerned about certain curricular materials and topics for study. What is considered *controversial subject matter,* as differentiated from a controversial issue, varies from college to college and community to community. Any issue or topic has the potential to become controversial at some time or place. Academic controversy is a procedure for learning; it is not specific subject matter, curricular material, or a topic.

Academic controversies create interest in subject matter and motivate students to investigate issues and points of

While the many advantages of controversy are apparent, it can be dangerous to engage students in a controversy under certain conditions.

view they would not ordinarily be interested in. Controversial issues and subject matter are just the opposite. They involve issues that students may be so emotionally involved in and feel so strongly about that a rational discussion is difficult. When unplanned and/or highly emotionally charged issues arise in a class, however, faculty need a procedure and plan for dealing with them.

Unplanned controversies

Unplanned controversies are often the result of information contributed in class that may not follow the content or direct line of learning the instructor has prepared. When unplanned controversies arise, the instructor should:

1. Give positive support to the student who raises the issue, unless it is distracting or irrelevant to the class.
2. Give the student an opportunity to define his or her position and identify the source of his or her information. All the rules of evidence and reasoned judgment apply.
3. Contact the department chair or appropriate administrator, if the topic clearly reflects a community sensitivity, to explain in advance the plans to discuss it. The feelings and beliefs of the people in the community should be considered as the topic is discussed.
4. Tell the librarian or media specialist about the topic to be discussed so he or she can locate and make available useful reference material.
5. Use the procedure for academic controversy to structure and conduct the discussion.
6. Emphasize the skills of focusing on the issue and not attacking or criticizing the person who raised the idea.
7. When the discussion is complete, relate the importance of the topic and its discussion to the original purpose of the class so students can see the significance of the topic to the course material.

Learning how to be a citizen in a democracy

The word "democracy" comes from the Greek *demokratia*, which is a combination of *demos* (Greek for "people") and *kratos* (Greek for "rule"). One of the most impressive democracies the world has ever seen existed in the city of Athens. At its height in the fifth century B.C., Athens had an assembly of all citizens that met 10 times a year for an open exchange of ideas and opinions. Between such meetings, a council of 500 citizens elected annually did most of the important government work. Thomas Jefferson, who admired Athenian democracy, believed that free and open discussion, not the social rank a person has been born into, should serve as the basis of influence in society. Jefferson was fond of noting that the first kings of Greece were elected by the free consent of the people. He was also influenced by one of his professors at William and Mary College, Dr. William Small of Scotland. Small advocated a new method of learning in which students questioned and discussed, examining all sides of a topic, with scant regard for the pronouncements of established authorities. A few years before his death, Thomas Jefferson described his experiences as a student at William and Mary in a letter to Dr. Thomas Cooper: "I was bold in the pursuit of knowledge, never fearing to follow the truth and reason to whatever results they led, and bearding every authority which stood in the way."

Based on the beliefs of Thomas Jefferson and his fellow revolutionaries, American democracy was founded on the premise that "truth" will result from free and open discussion in which opposing points of view are advocated and vigorously argued. In this country, we encourage rather than suppress the expression of opposing views because we have faith that truth will arise from the uninhibited clash of opposing views. Before a decision is made, every citizen is given the opportunity to advocate his or her ideas. Once a decision is made, the minority are expected to willingly support the majority because they know they have been given a fair and complete hearing. To be a citizen in our democracy, individuals need to master the process of advocating their views, challenging opposing positions, making a decision, and committing themselves to implement the decision made (regardless of their initial position).

Looking Forward

Thomas Jefferson based his faith in the future on the power of constructive conflict. Although numerous theorists have advocated the use of intellectual conflict in instructional situations, instructors have been reluctant to do so, perhaps because of a cultural fear of conflict, lack of knowledge of procedures, and cultural and pedagogical norms discouraging the use of conflict. But academic controversy provides a clear procedure for faculty to use in promoting intellectual conflicts. Strong research indicates that academic controversy results in many positive benefits for students, including higher achievement, more positive relationships with classmates, and increased self-esteem. Numerous research studies have validated the process by which controversy works. The instructor's role in conducting an academic controversy involves making a number of decisions before beginning instruction, explaining the task and the controversy procedure, monitoring the effectiveness of the controversy procedure, and evaluating students' achievement.

1. *Research and prepare a position.* Each pair takes an assigned position, gathers evidence to support it, organizes the evidence into a logical structure that provides a rationale for the position, plans how to advocate it forcefully and persuasively, and seeks as complete an intellectual understanding of the issue as current knowledge allows. A persuasive argument consists of a thesis statement, a rationale, and a conclusion. The rationale consists of the evidence arranged in a sequence involving an outline, a hierarchy, a causal network, or a web network. Once the evidence is organized, students use both inductive and deductive logic to derive the conclusion.

2. *Present and advocate the position.* Members of each pair make their presentation to members of the opposing pair. Students are to be as persuasive and convincing as possible. Members of the opposing pair are encouraged to take notes, listen carefully to learn the information being presented, and clarify anything they do not understand.

3. *Refute the opposing position and rebut attacks on your own.* Students argue forcefully and persuasively for their position, presenting as many facts as they can to support their point of view. Group members analyze and critically evaluate the opposing pair's information and inductive and deductive reasoning. They refute the opposing pair's arguments and rebut attacks on their own position. They discuss the issue, following a set of rules to help them criticize ideas without criticizing people, differentiate the two positions, and assess the degree of evidence and logic supporting each position.

4. *Reverse perspectives.* The pairs reverse perspectives and present each other's positions. In arguing for the opposing position, students are forceful and persuasive. They strive to see the issue from both perspectives simultaneously.

5. *Synthesize and integrate the best evidence and reasoning into a joint position.* The four members of the group drop all advocacy and synthesize and integrate what they know into factual and judgmental conclusions that are summarized into a joint position on which all sides can agree. Synthesizing is a creative process that involves seeing new patterns in a body of evidence, viewing the issue from a variety of perspectives, and creating a new position that subsumes the previous ones.

The skills required to implement this procedure are intellectual skills that all college students are well advised to develop sooner or later. Engaging in a controversy can be fun, enjoyable, and exciting.

The end of this monograph signals a new beginning. Years of experience in using academic controversy are needed to gain real expertise in managing intellectual conflicts constructively. The more students engage in the controversy process, the more they will learn, the more they will like each other, and the healthier they will be psychologically. It is through conflict that students grow, develop, learn, progress, and achieve. In the end, instructors will find that academic controversies enrich rather than disrupt life in the classroom.

REFERENCES

The Educational Resources Information Center (ERIC) Clearing-house on Higher Education abstracts and indexes the current literature on higher education for inclusion in ERIC's database and announcement in ERIC's monthly bibliographic journal, *Resources in Education* (RIE). Most of these publications are available through the ERIC Document Reproduction Service (EDRS). For publications cited in this bibliography that are available from EDRS, ordering number and price code are included. Readers who wish to order a publication should write to the ERIC Document Reproduction Service, 3900 Wheeler Avenue, Alexandria, Virginia 22304. (Phone orders with VISA or MasterCard are taken at 800/227-ERIC or 703/823-0500.) When ordering, please specify the document (ED) number. Documents are available as noted in microfiche (MF) and paper copy (PC). If you have the price code ready when you call, EDRS can quote an exact price. The last page of the latest issue of *Resources in Education* also has the current cost, listed by code.

Allen, V. 1965. "Situational Factors in Conformity." In *Advances in Experimental Social Psychology,* Vol. 2, edited by L. Berkowitz. New York: Academic Press.

———, ed. 1976. *Children as Teachers: Theory and Research on Tutoring.* New York: Academic Press.

Allport, G., and L. Postman. 1945. "The Basic Psychology of Rumor." *Translations of New York Academy of Sciences (Series 2)* 8: 61–81.

Ames, G., and F. Murray. 1982. "When Two Wrongs Make a Right: Promoting Cognitive Change by Social Conflict." *Developmental Psychology* 18: 892–95.

Anderson, N., and C. Graesser. 1976. "An Information Integration Analysis of Attitude Change in Group Discussion." *Journal of Personality and Social Psychology* 34: 210–22.

Annis, L. 1983. "The Processes and Effects of Peer Tutoring." *Human Learning* 2: 39–47.

Argyris, C. 1964. *Integrating the Individual and the Organization.* New York: Wiley.

Asch, S. 1952. *Social Psychology.* Englewood Cliffs, N.J.: Prentice-Hall.

———. 1956. "Studies of Independence and Conformity: A Minority of One against a Unanimous Majority." *Psychological Monographs* 70: 416.

Bach, G., and P. Wyden. 1969. *The Intimate Enemy.* New York: William Morrow.

Bahn, C. 1964. "The Interaction of Creativity and Social Facilitation in Creative Problem Solving." Doctoral dissertation, Columbia Univ.

Bargh, J., and Y. Schul. 1980. "On the Cognitive Benefits of Teaching." *Journal of Education Psychology* 72(5): 593–604.

Bartlett, F. 1932. *Remembering.* Cambridge, Eng.: Cambridge Univ. Press.

Beach, L. 1974. "Self-directed Student Group and College Learning." *Higher Education* 3: 187–200.

Beilin, H. 1977. "Inducing Conservation through Training." In *Psychology of the 20th Century: Piaget and Beyond,* Vol. 7, edited by G. Steiner. Zurich: Kindler.

Benware, C. 1975. "Quantitative and Qualitative Learning Differences as a Function of Learning in Order to Teach Another." Unpublished manuscript, Univ. of Rochester.

Berlyne, D. 1957. "Uncertainty and Conflict: A Point of Contact between Information Theory and Behavior Theory Concepts." *Psychological Review* 64: 329–39.

———. 1960. *Conflict, Arousal, and Curiosity.* New York: McGraw-Hill.

———. 1963. "Exploratory and Epistemic Behavior." In *Psychology: A Study of Science,* Vol. 5, edited by S. Koch. New York: McGraw-Hill.

———. 1965. "Curiosity and Education." In *Learning and the Educational Process,* edited by J. Krumboltz. Chicago: Rand McNally.

———. 1966. "Notes on Intrinsic Motivation and Intrinsic Reward in Relation to Instruction." In *Learning about Learning,* edited by J. Bruner. Cooperative Research Monograph No. 15. Washington, D.C.: U.S. Dept. of Health, Education, and Welfare, Office of Education. ED 015 492. 280 pp. MF–01; PC not available EDRS.

———. 1971. *Aesthetics and Psychobiology.* New York: Appleton-Century-Crofts.

Bigelow, R. 1972. "The Evolution of Cooperation, Aggression, and Self-Control." In *Nebraska Symposium on Motivation,* edited by J.K. Cole and D.D. Jensen. Lincoln: Univ. of Nebraska Press.

Blake, R., and J. Mouton. 1969. *Building a Dynamic Corporation through Grid Organization and Development.* Reading, Mass.: Addison-Wesley.

Blatt, M. 1969. "The Effects of Classroom Discussion upon Children's Level of Moral Judgment." Doctoral dissertation, Univ. of Chicago.

Blatt, M., and L. Kohlberg. 1973. "The Effects of Classroom Moral Discussion upon Children's Level of Moral Judgment." In *Collected Papers on Moral Development and Moral Education,* edited by L. Kohlberg. Cambridge, Mass.: Harvard Univ., Moral Education and Research Foundation.

Bolen, L., and E. Torrance. 1976. "An Experimental Study of the Influence of Locus of Control, Dyadic Interaction, and Sex on Creative Thinking." Paper presented at a meeting of the American Educational Research Association, April, San Francisco, California.

Borys, S., and H. Spitz. 1979. "Effect of Peer Interaction on the Problem-solving Behavior of Mentally Retarded Youths." *American Journal of Mental Deficiency* 84(3): 273–79.

Botvin, G., and F. Murray. 1975. "The Efficacy of Peer Modeling and Social Conflict in the Acquisition of Conversation." *Child Development* 46(3): 796–99.

Boulding, E. 1964. "Further Reflections on Conflict Management." In *Power and Conflict in Organizations,* edited by R. Kahn and E. Boulding. New York: Basic Books.

Bruner, J. 1961. *The Process of Education.* Cambridge, Mass.: Harvard Univ. Press.

Bruner, J., and A. Minturn. 1955. "Perceptual Identification and Perceptual Organization." *Journal of Genetic Psychology* 53: 21–28.

Burdick, H., and A. Burnes. 1958. "A Test of 'Strain toward Symmetry' Theories." *Journal of Abnormal and Social Psychology* 57: 367–69.

Collins, B. 1970. *Social Psychology.* Reading, Mass.: Addison-Wesley.

Cook, H., and F. Murray. 1973. "Acquisition of Conservation through the Observation of Conserving Models." Paper presented at a meeting of the American Educational Research Association, February, New Orleans, Louisiana. ED 080 210. 8 pp. MF–01; PC–01.

Coser, L. 1956. *The Function of Social Conflict.* Glencoe, Ill.: Free Press.

Crockenberg, S., and J. Nicolayev. 1977. "Stage Transition in Moral Reasoning as Related to Conflict Experienced in Naturalistic Settings." Paper presented at a meeting of the Society for Research in Child Development, March, New Orleans, Louisiana.

Dearborn, C., and H. Simon. 1958. "Selective Perception: A Note on the Departmental Identification of Executives." *Sociometry* 23: 667–73.

Deutsch, M. 1962. "Cooperation and Trust: Some Theoretical Notes." In *Nebraska Symposium on Motivation,* edited by M. Jones. Lincoln: Univ. of Nebraska Press.

―――. 1969. "Conflicts: Productive and Destructive." *Journal of Social Issues* 25: 7–43.

―――. 1973. *The Resolution of Conflict*. New Haven, Conn.: Yale Univ. Press.

―――. 1994. "Constructive Conflict Resolution: Principles, Training, and Research." *Journal of Social Issues* 50(1): 13–32.

Deutsch, M., and H. Gerard. 1955. "A Study of Normative and Informational Social Influences upon Individual Judgment." *Journal of Abnormal and Social Psychology* 51: 629–36.

DeVries, D., and K. Edwards. 1973. "Learning Games and Student Teams: Their Effects on Classroom Process." *American Educational Research Journal* 10(4): 307–18.

Doise, W., and G. Mugny. 1979. "Individual and Collective Conflicts of Centrations in Cognitive Development." *European Journal of Social Psychology* 9: 105–8.

Doise, W., G. Mugny, and A. Perret-Clermont. 1976. "Social Interaction and Cognitive Development: Further Evidence." *European Journal of Social Psychology* 6: 245–47.

Dunnette, M., J. Campbell, and K. Jaastad. 1963. "The Effect of Group Participation on Brainstorming Effectiveness of Two Industrial Samples." *Journal of Applied Psychology* 47: 30–37.

Dunning, D., and L. Ross. 1988. "Overconfidence in Individual and Group Prediction: Is the Collective Any Wiser?" Unpublished manuscript, Cornell Univ.

Falk, D., and D.W. Johnson. 1977. "The Effects of Perspective Taking and Egocentrism on Problem Solving in Heterogeneous and Homogeneous Groups." *Journal of Social Psychology* 102: 63–72.

Feffer, M., and L. Suchotliff. 1966. "Decentering Implications of Social Interaction." *Journal of Personality and Social Psychology* 4: 415–22.

Festinger, L., and N. Maccoby. 1964. "On Resistance to Persuasive Communications." *Journal of Abnormal and Social Psychology* 68: 359–66.

Fiedler, F., W. Meuwese, and S. Oonk. 1961. "An Exploratory Study of Group Creativity in Laboratory Tasks." *Acta Psychology* 18: 100–19.

Fisher, R. 1969. "An 'Each One Teach One' Approach to Music Notation." *Grade Teacher* 86(6): 120.

Flavell, J. 1963. *The Developmental Psychology of Jean Piaget*. Princeton, N.J.: Van Nostrand.

―――. 1968. *The Development of Role-taking and Communication Skills in Children*. New York: Wiley.

Foley, J., and F. MacMillan. 1943. "Mediated Generalization and the

Interpretation of Verbal Behavior. Part V. Free Association as Related to Differences in Professional Training." *Journal of Experimental Psychology* 33: 299–310.

Follet, M. 1940. "Constructive Conflict." In *Dynamic Administration: The Collected Papers of Mary Parker Follet,* edited by H. Metcalf and L. Urwick. New York: Harper.

Freud, S. 1930. *Civilization and Its Discontents.* London: Horgarth.

Frick, F. 1973. *Study of Peer Training with the Lincoln Training System.* AFATC Report KE 73-116. Harrison, Miss.: Keesler Air Force Base.

Gartner, A., M. Kohler, and F. Reissman. 1971. *Children Teach Children: Learning by Teaching.* New York: Harper & Row.

Gelman, R. 1978. "Cognition Development." *Annual Review of Psychology* 29: 297–332.

Gerard, H., and C. Greenbaum. 1962. "Attitudes toward and Agent of Uncertainty Reduction." *Journal of Personality* 30: 485–95.

Glidewell, J. 1953. "Group Emotionality and Production." Doctoral dissertation, Univ. of Chicago.

Gmelch, W.H. 1991. "The Creation of Constructive Conflict within Educational Administration Departments." Paper presented at an annual meeting of the University Council for Educational Administration, October, Baltimore, Maryland. ED 339 123. 33 pp. MF–01; PC–02.

Goldman, M. 1965. "A Comparison of Individual and Group Performance for Varying Combinations of Initial Ability." *Journal of Personality and Social Psychology* 1: 210–16.

Greenwald, A., and R. Albert. 1968. "Acceptance and Recall of Improvised Arguments." *Journal of Personality and Social Psychology* 8: 31–35.

Guilford, J. 1956. "The Structure of Intellect." *Psychological Bulletin* 33: 267–93.

Gunderson, B., and D.W. Johnson. 1980. "Building Positive Attitudes by Using Cooperative Learning Groups." *Foreign Language Annals* 13(1): 39–46.

Hall, J., and M. Williams. 1966. "A Comparison of Decision-making Performance in Established Ad Hoc Groups." *Journal of Personality and Social Psychology* 3: 214–222.

———. 1970. "Group Dynamics Training and Improved Decision Making." *Journal of Applied Behavioral Science* 6: 39–68.

Hammond, K. 1965. "New Directions in Research on Conflict Resolution." *Journal of Social Issues* 11: 44–66.

Hammond, K., and P. Boyle. 1971. "Quasi-rationality, Quarrels, and New Conceptions of Feedback." *Bulletin of the British Psycho-*

logical Society 24: 103–13.

Hoffman, L., E. Harburg, and N. Maier. 1962. "Differences in Disagreements as Factors in Creative Problem Solving." *Journal of Abnormal and Social Psychology* 64: 206–14.

Hoffman, L., and N. Maier. 1961. "Sex Differences, Sex Composition, and Group Problem Solving." *Journal of Abnormal and Social Psychology* 63: 453–56.

Hogan, R., and N. Henley. 1970. "A Test of the Empathy–Effective Communication Hypothesis." Report No. 84. Baltimore: Johns Hopkins Univ., Center for Social Organization of Schools. ED 043 642. MF–01; PC–01.

Hovey, D., H. Gruber, and G. Terrell. 1963. "Effects of Self-directed Study on Course Achievement, Retention, and Curiosity." *Journal of Educational Research* 56(7): 346–51.

Hunt, J. 1964. "Introduction: Revisiting Montessori." In *The Montessori Method,* edited by M. Montessori. New York: Shocken Books.

Inagaki, K. 1981. "Facilitation of Knowledge Integration through Classroom Discussion." *Quarterly Newsletter of the Laboratory of Comparative Human Cognition* 3: 26–28.

Inagaki, K., and G. Hatano. 1968. "Motivational Influences on Epistemic Observation." *Japanese Journal of Educational Psychology* 16: 221–28.

———. 1977. "Amplification of Cognitive Motivation and Its Effects on Epistemic Observation." *American Educational Research Journal* 14(4): 485–91.

Inhelder, B., and H. Sinclair. 1969. "Learning Cognitive Structures." In *Trends and Issues in Developmental Psychology,* edited by P. Mussen, J. Langer, and M. Covington. New York: Holt, Rinehart & Winston.

Iverson, M., and H. Schwab. 1967. "Ethnocentric Dogmatism and Binocular Fusion of Sexually and Racially Discrepant Stimuli." *Journal of Personality and Social Psychology* 7: 73–81.

Janis, I. 1982. *Groupthink: Psychological Studies of Policy Decisions and Fiascoes.* Boston: Houghton Mifflin.

Johnson, D.W. 1970. *Social Psychology of Education.* New York: Holt.

———. 1971a. "Role Reversal: A Summary and Review of the Research." *International Journal of Group Tensions* 1: 318–34.

———. 1971b. "Students against the School Establishment: Crisis Intervention in School Conflicts and Organization Change." *Journal of School Psychology* 9(1): 84–92.

———. 1973. *Contemporary Social Psychology.* Philadelphia: Lippincott.

————. 1974. "Communication and the Inducement of Cooperative Behavior in Conflicts: A Critical Review." *Speech Monographs* 41(1): 64–78.

————. 1975a. "Affective Perspective Taking and Cooperative Pre-disposition." *Developmental Psychology* 11(6): 869–70.

————. 1975b. "Cooperativeness and Social Perspective Taking." *Journal of Personality and Social Psychology* 31: 241–44.

————. 1977. "Distribution and Exchange of Information in Problem-solving Dyads." *Communication Research* 4(3): 283–98.

————. 1979. *Educational Psychology.* Englewood Cliffs, N.J.: Prentice-Hall.

————. 1980. "Group Processes: Influences of Student-Student Interaction on School Outcomes." In *The Social Psychology of School Learning,* edited by J. McMillam. New York: Academic Press.

————. 1991. *Human Relations and Your Career.* 3d ed. (1st ed. 1978). Englewood Cliffs, N.J.: Prentice-Hall.

————. 1997. *Reaching Out: Interpersonal Effectiveness and Self-Actualization.* 6th ed. (1st ed. 1971). Englewood Cliffs, N.J.: Prentice-Hall.

Johnson, D.W., and F. Johnson. 1975. *Joining Together: Group Theory and Group Skills.* Englewood Cliffs, N.J.: Prentice-Hall.

————. 1997. *Joining Together: Group Theory and Group Skills.* 6th ed. Englewood Cliffs, N.J.: Prentice-Hall.

Johnson, D.W., F. Johnson, and R. Johnson. 1976. "Promoting Constructive Conflict in the Classroom." *Notre Dame Journal of Education* 7(2): 163–68.

Johnson, D.W., and R. Johnson. 1974. "Instructional Goal Structure: Cooperative, Competitive, or Individualistic." *Review of Educational Research* 44(2): 213–40.

————. 1979. "Conflict in the Classroom: Controversy and Learning." *Review of Educational Research* 49(1): 51–69.

————. 1983. "The Socialization and Achievement Crises: Are Cooperative Learning Experiences the Solution?" In *Applied Social Psychology Annual 4,* edited by L. Bickman. Beverly Hills, Calif.: Sage.

————. 1984. "Building Acceptance of Differences between Handicapped and Nonhandicapped Students: The Effects of Cooperative and Individualistic Problems." *Journal of Social Psychology* 122: 257–67.

————. 1985. "Classroom Conflict: Controversy versus Debate in Learning Groups." *American Educational Research Journal* 22:

237–56.

———. 1987. *Creative Conflict*. Edina, Minn.: Interaction Book Co.

———. May 1988a. "Critical Thinking through Structured Controversy." *Educational Leadership* 45(8): 58–64.

———. 1988b. "Teaching Students to Manage Conflict Constructively by Involving Them in Academic Controversies." Paper presented at an annual meeting of the American Association for the Advancement of Science, February.

———. 1989. *Cooperation and Competition: Theory and Research.* Edina, Minn.: Interaction Book Co.

———. 1992a. "Encouraging Thinking through Constructive Controversy." In *Enhancing Thinking through Cooperative Learning,* edited by N. Davidson and T. Worsham. New York: Teachers College Press.

———. 1992b. "Pro–Con: Structuring Academic Controversy." In *Cooperative Learning: Making It Work in Social Studies,* edited by R. Stahl. Boston: Addison-Wesley.

———. 1993. "Creative and Critical Thinking through Academic Controversy." *American Behavioral Scientist* 37(1): 40–53.

———. 1994a. *Leading the Cooperative School.* 2d ed. Edina, Minn.: Interaction Book Co.

———. 1994b. *Learning Together and Alone: Cooperative, Competitive, and Individualistic Learning.* 4th ed. (1st ed. 1975). Englewood Cliffs, N.J.: Prentice-Hall.

———. 1995a. *Creative Controversy: Intellectual Challenge in the Classroom.* Edina, Minn.: Interaction Book Co.

———. 1995b. *Teaching Students to Be Peacemakers.* Edina, Minn.: Interaction Book Co.

Johnson, D.W., R. Johnson, and E. Holubec. 1993a. *Circles of Learning: Cooperation in the Classroom.* 4th ed. Edina, Minn.: Interaction Book Co.

———. 1993b. *Cooperation in the Classroom.* 5th ed. Edina, Minn.: Interaction Book Co.

Johnson, D.W., R. Johnson, W. Pierson, and V. Lyons. 1985. "Controversy versus Concurrence Seeking in Multigrade and Single-grade Learning Groups." *Journal of Research in Science Teaching* 22(9): 835–48.

Johnson, D.W., R. Johnson, and L. Scott. 1978. "Effects of Cooperative and Individualized Instruction on Student Attitudes and Achievement." *Journal of Social Psychology* 104: 207–16.

Johnson, D.W., R. Johnson, and K. Smith. 1989. "Controversy within Decision-making Situations." In *Managing Conflict: An Interdisciplinary Approach,* edited by M. Rahim. New York:

Praeger.

————. 1991. *Active Learning: Cooperation in the College Classroom.* Edina, Minn.: Interaction Book Co.

Johnson, D.W., R. Johnson, and M. Tiffany. 1984. "Structuring Academic Conflicts between Majority and Minority Students: Hindrance or Help to Integration?" *Contemporary Educational Psychology* 9(1): 61–73.

Johnson, R., C. Brooker, J. Stutzman, D. Hultman, and D.W. Johnson. 1985. "The Effects of Controversy, Concurrence Seeking, and Individualistic Learning on Achievement and Attitude Change." *Journal of Research in Science Teaching* 22(3): 197–205.

Jones, E., and J. Aneshansel. 1956. "The Learning and Utilization of Contravaluant Material." *Journal of Abnormal and Social Psychology* 53: 27–33.

Judd, C. 1978. "Cognitive Effects of Attitude Conflict Resolution." *Journal of Conflict Resolution* 22: 483–98.

Kalven, H., and H. Zeisel. 1966. *The American Jury.* Boston: Little & Brown.

Kaplan, M. 1977. "Discussion Polarization Effects in a Modern Jury Decision Paradigm: Informational Influences." *Sociometry* 40: 262–71.

Kaplan, M., and C. Miller. 1977. "Judgments and Group Discussion: Effect of Presentation and Memory Factors on Polarization." *Sociometry* 40: 337–43.

Keasey, C. 1973. "Experimentally Induced Changes in Moral Opinions and Reasoning." *Journal of Personality and Social Psychology* 226: 30–38.

Kleinhesselink, R., and R. Edwards. 1975. "Seeking and Avoiding Belief-discrepant Information as a Function of Its Perceived Refutability." *Journal of Personality and Social Psychology* 31: 787–90.

Knight-Arest, I., and D. Reid. 1977. "Peer Interaction as a Catalyst for Conservation Acquisition in Normal and Learning-disabled Children." Paper presented at the Eighth Annual Symposium of the Jean Piaget Society, May, Philadelphia, Pennsylvania. ED 162 489. 14 pp. MF–01; PC–01.

Kohlberg, L. 1969. "Stage and Sequence: The Cognitive-Developmental Approach to Socialization." In *Handbook of Socialization Theory and Research,* edited by D. Goslin. Chicago: Rand McNally.

Kuhn, D., J. Langer, L. Kohlberg, and N. Haan. 1977. "The Development of Formal Operations in Logical and Moral Judgment."

Genetic Psychological Monographs 55: 97–188.

Langer, E., A. Blank, and B. Chanowitz. 1978. "The Mindlessness of Ostensibly Thoughtful Action: The Role of 'Placebic' Information in Interpersonal Interaction." *Journal of Personality and Social Psychology* 36(6): 635–42.

Laughlin, P. 1980. "Social Combination Processes of Cooperative Problem-solving Groups on Verbal Intellective Tasks." In *Progress in Social Psychology,* Vol. 1, edited by M. Fishbein. Hillsdale, N.J.: Erlbaum.

Laughlin, P., and J. Adamopoulos. 1980. "Social Combination Processes and Individual Learning for Six-person Cooperative Groups on an Intellective Task." *Journal of Personality and Social Psychology* 38: 941–47.

Laughlin, P., L. Branch, and H. Johnson. 1969. "Individual versus Triadic Performance on a Unidimensional Complementary Task as a Function of Initial Ability Level." *Journal of Personality and Social Psychology* 12: 144–50.

LeCount, J., J. Evens, and G. Maruyama. 1992. "It's a Tough World out There—for Men: Students' Attitudes toward Gender Socialization Pressures Following a Constructive Controversy." Paper presented at an annual meeting of the American Educational Research Association, April, San Francisco, California.

LeCount, J., G. Maruyama, R. Petersen, and F. Basset. 1991. "Minority Empowerment Strategies and Group Decision-making Processes." Paper presented at an annual meeting of the American Educational Research Association, April, Chicago, Illinois.

LeFurgy, W., and G. Woloshin. 1969. "Immediate and Long-term Effects of Experimentally Induced Social Influence in the Modification of Adolescents' Moral Judgments." *Journal of Personality and Social Psychology* 12: 104–10.

Levine, J., and G. Murphy. 1943. "The Learning and Forgetting of Controversial Material." *Journal of Abnormal and Social Psychology* 38: 507–17.

Levine, R., I. Chein, and G. Murphy. 1942. "The Relation of the Intensity of a Need to the Amount of Perceptual Distortion: A Preliminary Report." *Journal of Psychology* 13: 283–93.

Lord, C., L. Ross, and M. Lepper. 1979. "Biased Assimilation and Attitude Polarization: The Effects of Prior Theories on Subsequently Considered Evidence." *Journal of Personality and Social Psychology* 37: 2098–109.

Lowin, A. 1969. "Further Evidence for an Approach-Avoidance Interpretation of Selective Exposure." *Journal of Experimental Social Psychology* 5: 265–71.

Lowry, N., and D.W. Johnson. 1981. "Effects of Controversy on Epistemic Curiosity, Achievement, and Attitudes." *Journal of Social Psychology* 115: 31–43.

Luchins, A. 1942. "Mechanization in Problem Solving: The Effect of *Einstellung.*" *Psychological Monographs* 54(6).

Lund, S. 1980. "Group Decision Making: The Effects of Controversy and Systematic Evaluation on Vigilant Information Processing." Doctoral dissertation, Univ. of Minnesota.

Maass, A., and R. Clark. 1984. "Hidden Impact of Minorities: Fifteen Years of Minority Influence Research." *Psychological Bulletin* 95: 428–50.

McClelland, D., and J. Atkinson. 1948. "The Projective Expression of Needs: I. The Effect of Different Intensities of the Hunger Drive on Perception." *Journal of Psychology* 25: 205–22.

Magnuson, E. 10 March 1986. "A Serious Deficiency: The Rogers Commission Faults NASA's Flawed Decision-making Process." *Time* (international ed.): 40–42.

Maier, N. 1930. "Reasoning in Humans." *Journal of Comparative Psychology* 10: 115–43.

———. 1970. *Problem Solving and Creativity in Individuals and Groups.* Belmont, Calif.: Brooks/Cole.

Maier, N., and L. Hoffman. 1964. "Financial Incentives and Group Decision in Motivating Change." *Journal of Social Psychology* 64: 369–78.

Maier, N., and A. Solem. 1952. "The Contributions of a Discussion Leader to the Quality of Group Thinking: The Effective Use of Minority Opinions." *Human Relations* 5: 277–88.

Maitland, D., and J. Goldman. 1974. "Moral Judgment as a Function of Peer Group Interaction." *Journal of Personality and Social Psychology* 30(5): 699–704.

Miller, S., and C. Brownell. 1975. "Peers, Persuasion, and Piaget: Dyadic Interaction between Conservers and Nonconservers." *Child Development* 46: 992–97.

Mitchell, J.M. 1997. "The Impact of Structured Controversy versus Concurrence Seeking in AIDS, Alcohol Abuse, and Cigarette Smoking Education." Ph.D. dissertation, Univ. of Minnesota.

Moscovici, S., and C. Faucheaux. 1972. "Social Influence, Conformity Bias, and the Study of Active Minorities." In *Advances in Experimental Social Psychology,* Vol. 6, edited by L. Berkowitz. New York: Academic Press.

Moscovici, S., and E. Lage. 1976. "Studies in Social Influence III: Majority versus Minority Influence in a Group." *European Journal of Social Psychology* 6: 149–74.

Moscovici, S., E. Lage, and M. Naffrechoux. 1969. "Influence of a Consistent Minority on the Responses of a Majority in a Color Perception Task." *Sociometry* 32: 365–80.

Moscovici, S., and C. Nemeth. 1974. "Social Influence II: Minority Influence." In *Social Psychology: Classic and Contemporary Integrations,* edited by C. Nemeth. Chicago: Rand McNally.

Mugny, G. 1980. *The Power of Minorities.* London: Academic Press.

Mugny, G., and W. Doise. 1978. "Sociocognitive Conflict and Structure of Individual and Collective Performers." *European Journal of Social Psychology* 8: 181–92.

Murray, F. 1972. "Acquisition of Conservation through Social Interaction." *Development of Psychology* 6: 1–6.

———. 1978. "Development of Intellect and Reading." In *The Acquisition of Reading,* edited by F. Murray and J. Pikulski. Baltimore: University Park Press.

———. 1981. "The Conservation Paradigm: Conservation of Conservation Research." In *New Directions in Piagetian Theory and Research,* edited by D. Brodzinsky, I. Sigel, and R. Golinkoff. Hillsdale, N.J.: Erlbaum.

———. 1982. "Teaching through Social Conflict." *Contemporary Educational Psychology* 7: 257–71.

———. 1983. "Cognitive Benefits of Teaching on the Teacher." Paper presented at an annual meeting of the American Educational Research Association, Montreal, Quebec.

Murray, F., G. Ames, and G. Botvin. 1977. "Acquisition of Conservation through Cognitive Dissonance." *Journal of Educational Psychology* 69(5): 519–27.

Murray, J. 1974. "Social Learning and Cognitive Development: Modeling Effects on Children's Understanding of Conservation." *British Journal of Psychology* 65(1): 151–60.

Neisser, U. 1954. "On Experimental Distinction between Perceptual Process and Verbal Response." *Journal of Experimental Psychology* 47: 399–402.

Nel, G., R. Helmreich, and E. Aronson. 1969. "Opinion Change in the Advocate as a Function of the Persuasibility of His Audience: A Clarification of the Meaning of Dissonance." *Journal of Personality and Social Psychology* 12: 117–24.

Nemeth, C. 1976. "A Comparison between Conformity and Minority Influence." Paper presented at a meeting of the International Congress of Psychology, Paris, France.

———. 1986. "Differential Contributions of Majority and Minority Influence." *Psychological Review* 93(1): 23–32.

Nemeth, C., and J. Kwan. 1985. "Originality of Word Associations as a Function of Majority versus Minority Influence." *Social Psychology Quarterly* 48: 277–82.

———. 1987. "Minority Influence, Divergent Thinking, and Detection of Correct Solutions." *Journal of Applied Social Psychology* 17: 788–99.

Nemeth, C., O. Mayseless, J. Sherman, and Y. Brown. 1990. "Exposure to Dissent and Recall of Information." *Journal of Personality and Social Psychology* 58: 429–37.

Nemeth, C., M. Swedlund, and B. Kanki. 1974. "Patterning of the Minorities' Responses and Their Influence on the Majority." *European Journal of Social Psychology* 4(1): 53–64.

Nemeth, C., and J. Wachtler. 1974. "Creating the Perceptions of Consistency and Confidence: A Necessary Condition for Minority Influence." *Sociometry* 37: 529–40.

———. 1983. "Creative Problem Solving as a Result of Majority versus Minority Influence." *European Journal of Social Psychology* 13(1): 45–55.

Nicholls, J. 1983. "Conceptions of Ability and Achievement Motivation: A Theory and Its Implications for Education." In *Learning and Motivation in the Classroom,* edited by S. Paris, G. Olson, and H. Stevenson. Hillsdale, N.J.: Erlbaum.

Nijhof, W., and P. Kommers. 1982. "Analysis of Cooperation in Relation to Cognitive Controversy." Paper presented at the Second International Conference on Cooperation in Education, July, Provo, Utah.

Nisbett, R., and L. Ross. 1980. *Human Inference: Strategies and Shortcomings of Social Judgment.* Englewood Cliffs, N.J.: Prentice-Hall.

Palmer, P. September/October 1987. "Community, Conflict, and Ways of Knowing." *Change:* 20–25.

———. January/February 1990. "Good Teaching: A Matter of Living the Mystery." *Change* 22(1): 11–16.

———. 1991. "The Courage to Teach." *National Teaching and Learning Forum* 1(2): 1–3.

Pepitone, A. 1950. "Motivational Effects in Social Perception." *Human Relations* 3: 57–76.

Perret-Clermont, A. 1980. *Social Interaction and Cognitive Development in Children.* London: Academic Press.

Peters, R., and E. Torrance. 1972. "Dyadic Interaction of Preschool Children and Performance on a Construction Task." *Psychological Reports* 30: 747–50.

Petersen, R., and M. Tiffany. 1983. "Instructional Strategies for Constructive Controversies." Paper presented at an annual meeting of the American Educational Research Association, April 11–15, Montreal, Quebec. ED 234 053. 20 pp. MF–01; PC–01.

Piaget, J. 1948. *The Moral Judgment of the Child.* 2d ed. Glencoe, Ill.: Free Press.

———. 1950. *The Psychology of Intelligence.* New York: Harcourt.

Postman, L., and D. Brown. 1952. "The Perceptual Consequences of Success and Failure." *Journal of Abnormal and Social Psychology* 47: 213–21.

Putnam, L., and P. Geist. 1985. "Argument in Bargaining: An Analysis of the Reasoning Process." *Southern Speech Communication Journal* 50(3): 225–45.

Rest, J., E. Turiel, and L. Kohlberg. 1969. "Relations between Level of Moral Judgment and Preference and Comprehension of the Moral Judgment of Others." *Journal of Personality* 37: 225–52.

Rogers, C. 1970. "Towards a Theory of Creativity." In *Readings in Creativity,* edited by P. Vernon. London: Penguin.

Sarbin, T. 1976. "Cross-age Tutoring and Social Identity." In *Children as Teachers: Theory and Research on Tutoring,* edited by V. Allen. New York: Academic Press.

Sigel, I., and F. Hooper, eds. 1968. *Logical Thinking in Children: Research Based on Piaget's Theory.* New York: Holt, Rinehart, Winston.

Silverman, I., and E. Geiringer. 1973. "Dyadic Interaction and Conservation Induction: A Test of Piaget's Equilibration Model." *Child Development* 44(4): 815–20.

Silverman, I., and J. Stone. 1972. "Modifying Cognitive Functioning through Participation in a Problem-solving Group." *Journal of Educational Psychology* 63(1): 603–8.

Simmel, G. 1955. *Conflict.* New York: Free Press.

Simon, H. 1976. *Administrative Behavior: A Study of Decision-making Processes in Administrative Organizations.* 3d ed. New York: Free Press.

Sinclair, H. 1969. "Developmental Psycho-linguistics." In *Studies in Cognitive Development: Essays in Honor of Jean Piaget,* edited by D. Elkind and J. Flavell. New York: Oxford Univ. Press.

Smedslund, J. 1961a. "The Acquisition of Conservation of Substance and Weight in Children: II. External Reinforcement of Conservation and Weight and of the Operations of Addition and Subtraction." *Scandinavian Journal of Psychology* 2: 71–84.

———. 1961b. "The Acquisition of Conservation of Substance and Weight in Children: III. Extinction of Conservation of Weight Acquired 'Normally' and by Means of Empirical Controls on Balance." *Scandinavian Journal of Psychology* 2: 85–87.

Smith, K., D.W. Johnson, and R. Johnson. 1981. "Can Conflict Be Constructive? Controversy versus Concurrence Seeking in Learning Groups." *Journal of Educational Psychology* 73(5): 651–63.

———. 1984. "Effects of Controversy on Learning in Cooperative Groups." *Journal of Social Psychology* 122: 199–209.

Snyder, M., and N. Cantor. 1979. "Testing Theories about Other People: The Use of Historical Knowledge." *Journal of Experimental Social Psychology* 15: 330–42.

Swann, W., and S. Reid. 1981. "Acquiring Self-knowledge: The Search for Feedback That Fits." *Journal of Personality and Social Psychology* 41: 1119–28.

Tanford, S., and S. Penrod. 1984. "Social Influence Model: A Formal Integration of Research on Majority and Minority Influence Processes." *Psychological Bulletin* 95: 189–225.

Taylor, S. 1980. "The Interface of Cognitive and Social Psychology." In *Cognition, Social Behavior, and the Environment,* edited by J. Harvey. Hillsdale, N.J.: Erlbaum.

Tjosvold, D. 1974. "Threat as a Low Person's Strategy for Bargaining: Social Farce and Tangible Outcomes." *International Journal of Group Tensions* 4: 494–510.

———. 1982. "Effects of Approach to Controversy on Superiors' Incorporation of Subordinates' Information in Decision Making." *Journal of Applied Psychology* 67: 189–93.

———. 1990. "Flight Crew Collaboration to Manage Safety Risks." *Group and Organizational Studies* 15: 177–91.

Tjosvold, D., and D. Deemer. 1980. "Effects of Controversy within a Cooperative or Competitive Context on Organizational Decision Making." *Journal of Applied Psychology* 65: 590–95.

Tjosvold, D., and D.W. Johnson. 1977. "The Effects of Controversy on Cognitive Perspective Taking." *Journal of Educational Psychology* 69(1): 679–85.

———. 1978. "Controversy within a Cooperative or Competitive Context and Cognitive Perspective Taking." *Contemporary Educational Psychology* 3(4): 376–86.

———, eds. 1983. *Productive Conflict Management: Perspectives for Organizations.* New York: Irvington.

Tjosvold, D., D.W. Johnson, and L. Fabrey. 1980. "The Effects of Controversy and Defensiveness on Cognitive Perspective Taking." *Psychological Reports* 47: 1043–53.

Tjosvold, D., D.W. Johnson, and J. Lerner. 1981. "Effects of Affirmation of One's Competence, Personal Acceptance, and Disconfirmation of One's Competence on Incorporation of Opposing Information on Problem-solving Situations." *Journal of Social*

Psychology 114: 103–10.

Torrance, E. 1961. "Can a Group Control Social Stress in Creative Activity?" *Elementary School Journal* 62: 139–394.

———. 1970. "Influence of Dyadic Interaction on Creative Functioning." *Psychological Reports* 26(2): 391–94.

———. 1971. "Stimulation, Enjoyment, and Originality in Dyadic Creativity." *Journal of Educational Psychology* 62(1): 45–48.

———. 1973. "Dyadic Interaction in Creative Thinking and Problem Solving." Paper read at a meeting of the American Educational Research Association, February, New Orleans, Louisiana.

Triandis, H., A. Bass, R. Ewen, and E. Midesele. 1963. "Teaching Creativity as a Function of the Creativity of the Members." *Journal of Applied Psychology* 47: 104–10.

Turiel, E. 1966. "An Experimental Test of the Sequentiality of Developmental Stages in the Child's Moral Judgment." *Journal of Personality and Social Psychology* 3: 611–18.

———. 1973. "Stage Transition in Moral Development." In *Second Handbook of Research on Teaching,* edited by R. Travers. Chicago: Rand McNally.

Tversky, A., and D. Kahneman. 1981. "The Framing of Decisions and the Psychology of Choice." *Science* 211(4481): 453–58.

Van Blerkom, M., and D. Tjosvold. 1981. "The Effects of Social Context on Engaging in Controversy." *Journal of Psychology* 107: 141–45.

Vinokur, A., and E. Burnstein. 1974. "Effects of Partially Shared Persuasive Arguments on Group-induced Shifts." *Journal of Personality and Social Psychology* 29: 305–15.

Wallach, L., and R. Sprott. 1964. "Inducing Number Conservation in Children." *Child Development* 35: 1057–71.

Wallach, L., A. Wall, and L. Anderson. 1967. "Number Conservation: The Roles of Reversibility, Addition-Subtraction, and Misleading Perceptual Cues." *Child Development* 38: 425–42.

Walton, R. 1987. *Interpersonal Peacemaking.* Reading, Mass.: Addison-Wesley.

Watson, G., and D.W. Johnson. 1972. *Social Psychology: Issues and Insights.* Philadelphia: Lippincott.

Webb, N. 1977. *Learning in Individual and Small Group Settings.* Technical Report No. 7. Arlington, Va.: Office of Naval Research, Personnel and Training, Research Programs Office. ED 151 699. 131 pp. MF–01; PC–06.

Woholwill, J., and R. Lowe. 1962. "Experimental Analysis of the Development of the Conservation of Numbers." *Child Development* 33: 153–67.

Worchel, P., and B. McCormick. 1963. "Self-concept and Dissonance Reduction." *Journal of Personality* 31: 589–99.

Zajonc, R. 1965. "Social Facilitation." *Science* 149: 269–72.

Zimbardo, P. 1965. "The Effect of Effort and Improvisation on Self-persuasion Produced by Role Playing." *Journal of Experimental Social Psychology* 1: 103–20.

INDEX

A

academic assistance
>providing of, 57

academic controversy
>misunderstandings of, 101–2
>preparations required from the instructor for, 104
>steps in engaging in, 104–5
>use of, 49–50
>what is, 3–7

academic objective in preinstructional preparations, 50

academic task
>explaining the, 52

achievement and retention, 14, 16

active learning techniques often receive negative evaluations, x

advocacy
>dropping of, 96
>importance in our society of, 77
>proper process of, 77

AIDA outline, 67

ambiguous claims, 83

analytical methods, 60

"and" relationships, 86

appealing to authority, 65

appealing to the longevity of the conclusion, 65

appeals to emotion, 83

Aristotle suggested resolving controversies by engaging in
>"deliberate discourse," 4

assigning roles in preinstructional preparations, 51–52

assigning students to groups in preinstructional preparations, 51

attitude change, 19

Average Effect Size in Meta-Analysis of Controversy Studies, 15

avoidance of conflict as an inhibiting value, ix

B

Bacon, Sir Francis, 71–72

behaviors
>specifying desired, 55–56

being challenged by a majority or minority, 29–31

being challenged by a valid or erroneous position, 31

being overloaded with opposing information, 28–29

best disposable cup as a sample problem, 11

Bruner (1961) proposed that conceptual conflict is necessary for
>discovery learning, 1

"but" relationships, 86

C

controversial subject matter, 101–2

controversy

broad categories of documented outcomes of, 14

competitive context of, 39–40

dangers of, 101

impact on cognitive and moral reasoning, 36–38

inevitability, 8

necessity for, 99–100

positive goal, resource interdependence and conflict of, 7

process of, 25

rules, 12

structuring, 53–55

theory, 13

value, 16–17

Controversy, Debate, and Concurrence Seeking process, 23–24

controversy promotes

greater learning motivation than concurrence seeking, 16

greater searches for more information, 32

higher-level reasoning, 17

social support from other students, 20

controversy skills

intervening to teach, 57–58

conversion as a means of majority influence, 29

cooperative context for conflicts, 47–49

creating a, 45–46

cooperative goal structure, 38–40

cooperative learning

discussion of, 48

co-orientation

need in How to Manage Controversy, 8–9

creativity, 17–18

credible alternative views

exposure results in better recall and use of information, 16

results in the generation of more novel solutions, 18

credible source lack, 83

cultural values inhibiting faculty

from encouraging students to enter in learning process, ix

D

debate definition, 6

deciding on the size of groups in pre instructional decisions and preparations, 50

deductive reasoning, 71–72

is it reliable, 84
is there sufficient, 84
evidence and a better conceptualization
        searching for further, 87
explaining and orchestrating the academic task, cooperative goal
        structure, and controversy procedure, 52

F

face-to-face promotive interaction in cooperative learning, 49
faculty
        knowledge needed to use academic controversies, 9
        must allow students become active participants in learning
                process, ix
fear as a reasons for conflict avoidance in college classes, 2
freedom to express independent opinions, 28

G

group functioned
        processing how well the, 58–59
group processing in cooperative learning, 49
groupthink, 6

H

heterogeneity among members, 40–41
hierarchy in creating a conceptual framework, 69, 70
higher-level reasoning
        controversy tends to promote, 17
higher-quality problem solving
        depends on conflict among group members, 1
How to Solve It: Analytically or Numerically? as sample problem, 60

I

ignorance of how to engage in intellectual conflict as a reason for
        conflict avoidance in college classes, 2
incorporating others' information and reasoning, 34–35
indices of epistemic curiosity, 32
individual accountability
        structuring, 55
        in cooperative learning, 48–49
individualistic learning, 6–7
        has neither interdependence nor intellectual conflict, 7
inductive reasoning, 71–72
inefficient use of class time as an inhibiting value, ix

---

inertia as reason for conflict avoidance in college classes, 3

information

    influence, 29

    organization and deriving conclusions, 24–26

    overload, 29

instructional methods comparison, 7

instructor's role in structuring academic controversies, 45

integration/synthesis, 89

intellectual conflicts avoidance, 2–3

intellectual disagreement

    lure of suppressing, 100–1

intergroup cooperation structuring, 56

interpersonal attraction among participants, 19–20

J

Jefferson, Thomas

    believed that free and open discussion should serve as the
        basis of influence in society, 103

    had deep faith in the value and productiveness of conflict, 1

joint position that everyone agrees with

    group members should remember that ultimate goal is, 88

joint rewards in cooperative learning, 48

K

Kohlberg (1969) adopted Piaget's formulation as an explanation

    for development of moral reasoning, 1. *See also* Piaget

    (1950)

L

leaping to a conclusion, 73

learning how to be a citizen in a democracy, 102–3

learning opposing positions and perspectives, 80

learning positions in structuring the controversy, 53

learning process

    students must become active participants in, ix

lesson

    providing closure to, 58

Lewin, Kurt

    authors' indebtedness to work of, xiii

Light: Particle or Wave? as a sample problem, 21

logical sequence creation, 71

longevity of the conclusion

    appealing to the, 65

M

Maier (1972) says higher-quality problem solving depends on
　　conflict among group members, 1

meaningless claims, 83

mental sets can cause the same words to have different meanings
　　for different persons, 25

Meta-Analysis of Controversy Studies
　　Average Effect Size in, 15

Michigan State University, 23

Milton, John
　　Doctrine and Discipline, 18

mind changing when logically persuaded to do so
　　group members should, 89

mind map in creating a conceptual framework, 69

minority influence, 30

misperceiving opposing information and reasoning, 28

modality
　　using more than one, 74

monitoring and intervening, 57–58

monitoring students' behavior, 57

moral reasoning
　　controversy impact on, 36–38

mutual learning goals in cooperative learning, 48

N

normative influence, 29

norms need shared expectations
　　about appropriate behavior in resolving conflict, 9

Novarum Organum, sive indicia vera de interpretatione naturae,
　　71–72

numerical methods, 60

O

open discussion of the issue, 80–81

opinion as but knowledge in the making, 18

opposing positions. seeking to understand, 33

organizing what is known into a reasoned position, 65–66

outline in creating a conceptual framework, 67

oversimplification of causal relationships, 83

P

Palmer (1990, 1991) believes that fear of conflict
　　blocks good teaching and learning, 2

pedagogical norms as reason for conflict avoidance
in college classes, 3
peers more effective in teaching information to their peers
than specially trained experts, 27
perceiving the usefulness of the opposing position, 29
perspective reversal, 93–95
perspective taking, 42, 93
value of, 94–95
persuasive argument three parts, 66
persuasive outline, 67
persuasive presentation guidelines, 78–79
Piaget (1950) disequilibrium in a student's cognitive structure
motivates transitions from stage of cognitive reasoning, 1
planning instructional materials to promote interdependence and
controversy in pre instructional decisions and preparations,
51
political correctness desire as an inhibiting value, ix
positive interdependence
in cooperative learning, 48
structuring, 52
PPF outline, 67
practicing, 74
preferred position or approach as an inhibiting value, ix
preinstructional decisions and preparations, 50–52
preparing
a position, 62–63
to present your position, 73
present and advocate a position, 5
presenting and advocating conclusions and rationale, 26–27
presenting positions in structuring the controversy, 53–54
presenting your position, 78–79
processing how well the group did, 58–59, 98
psychological health and social competence, 20–21
psychological theorization on processes through which conflict
leads to higher productivity, 23

Q
quality of problem solving, 16–17

R
reaching a decision in structuring the controversy, 54–55
rebutting attacks on one's own position, 86–87
reconceptualization, synthesis, and integration, 34

synthesize, 96–97
synthesizing and integrating, 95–96
        best evidence and reasoning into a joint position, 5–6

T
taking a perspective, 73–74
task involvement, 18–19
task orientation, 26
teacher's role in structuring controversies, 46
teaching techniques that deviate from the norm not highly valued,
        x
testing on issue, 97
"therefore" relationships, 86
Tjosvold, Dean
        authors' indebtedness to work of, xiii

U
uncertainty created by being challenged by opposing views, 27–28
University of Minnesota review of teaching style, x
unplanned controversies, 102
unwarranted assumptions, 85

V
vague claims, 83
Venn diagram in creating a conceptual framework, 69, 70
viewing the situation from different perspectives, 33–34

W
Web network in creating a conceptual framework, 67–68
Which Books Do We Take? as a sample problem, 90
William and Mary College, 103
writing a report, 97

ASHE-ERIC HIGHER EDUCATION REPORTS

Since 1983, the Association for the Study of Higher Education (ASHE) and the Educational Resources Information Center (ERIC) Clearinghouse on Higher Education, a sponsored project of the Graduate School of Education and Human Development at The George Washington University, have cosponsored the ASHE-ERIC Higher Education Report series. This volume is the twenty-fifth overall and the eighth to be published by the Graduate School of Education and Human Development at The George Washington University.

Each monograph is the definitive analysis of a tough higher education problem, based on thorough research of pertinent literature and institutional experiences. Topics are identified by a national survey. Noted practitioners and scholars are then commissioned to write the reports, with experts providing critical reviews of each manuscript before publication.

Eight monographs (10 before 1985) in the ASHE-ERIC Higher Education Report series are published each year and are available on individual and subscription bases. To order, use the order form on the last page of this book.

Qualified persons interested in writing a monograph for the ASHE-ERIC Higher Education Report series are invited to submit a proposal to the National Advisory Board. As the preeminent literature review and issue analysis series in higher education, the Higher Education Reports are guaranteed wide dissemination and national exposure for accepted candidates. Execution of a monograph requires at least a minimal familiarity with the ERIC database, including *Resources in Education* and the current *Index to Journals in Education*. The objective of these reports is to bridge conventional wisdom with practical research. Prospective authors are strongly encouraged to call Dr. Fife at 800-773-3742.

For further information, write to
ASHE-ERIC Higher Education Reports
The George Washington University
One Dupont Circle, Suite 630
Washington, DC 20036
Or phone (202) 296-2597; toll free: 800-773-ERIC.

Write or call for a complete catalog.

Visit our Web site at http://www.gwu.edu/~eriche

ADVISORY BOARD

James Earl Davis
University of Delaware at Newark

Cassie Freeman
Peabody College–Vanderbilt University

Susan Frost
Emory University

Mildred Garcia
Arizona State University West

James Hearn
University of Georgia

Philo Hutcheson
Georgia State University

CONSULTING EDITORS

Philip G. Altbach
State University of New York–Buffalo

Marilyn J. Amey
University of Kansas

Thomas A. Angelo
AAHE Assessment Forum

Louis C. Attinasi
Loyola University

Stewart Bellman
Black Hills State University

Steve Brigham
American Association for Higher Education

Ivy E. Broder
The American University

James Cooper
California State University–Dominguez Hills

Robert A. Cornesky
Cornesky and Associates, Inc.

Barbara Gross Davis
University of California at Berkeley

James R. Davis
Center for Academic Quality and Assessment of Student
    Learning

Cheryl Falk
Yakima Valley Community College

L. Dee Fink
University of Oklahoma

Anne II. Frank
American Association of University Professors

Joseph E. Gilmore
Northwest Missouri State University

Dean L. Hubbard
Northwest Missouri State University

Mardee Jenrette
Miami-Dade Community College

George D. Kuh
Indiana University

Diane E. Morrison
Centre for Curriculum and Professional Development

L. Jackson Newell
University of Utah

Steven G. Olswang
University of Washington

Brent Ruben
State University of New Jersey–Rutgers

Sherry Sayles-Folks
Eastern Michigan University

Daniel Seymour
Claremont College–California

Pamela D. Sherer
The Center for Teaching Excellence

David Sweet
OERI, U.S. Department of Education

Kathe Taylor
State of Washington Higher Education Coordinating Board

Gershon Vincow
Syracuse University

W. Allan Wright
Dalhousie University

Manta Yorke
Liverpool John Moores University

REVIEW PANEL

Charles Adams
University of Massachusetts–Amherst

Louis Albert
American Association for Higher Education

Richard Alfred
University of Michigan

Henry Lee Allen
University of Rochester

Philip G. Altbach
Boston College

Marilyn J. Amey
University of Kansas

Kristine L. Anderson
Florida Atlantic University

Karen D. Arnold
Boston College

Robert J. Barak
Iowa State Board of Regents

Alan Bayer
Virginia Polytechnic Institute and State University

John P. Bean
Indiana University–Bloomington

John M. Braxton
Peabody College, Vanderbilt University

Ellen M. Brier
Tennessee State University

Barbara E. Brittingham
The University of Rhode Island

Dennis Brown
University of Kansas

Peter McE. Buchanan
Council for Advancement and Support of Education

Patricia Carter
University of Michigan

John A. Centra
Syracuse University

Arthur W. Chickering
George Mason University

Darrel A. Clowes
Virginia Polytechnic Institute and State University

Cynthia S. Dickens
Mississippi State University

Deborah M. DiCroce
Piedmont Virginia Community College

Sarah M. Dinham
University of Arizona

Kenneth A. Feldman
State University of New York–Stony Brook

Dorothy E. Finnegan
The College of William & Mary

Mildred Garcia
Montclair State College

Rodolfo Z. Garcia
Commission on Institutions of Higher Education

Kenneth C. Green
University of Southern California

James Hearn
University of Georgia

Edward R. Hines
Illinois State University

Deborah Hunter
University of Vermont

Philo Hutcheson
Georgia State University

Bruce Anthony Jones
University of Pittsburgh

Elizabeth A. Jones
The Pennsylvania State University

Kathryn Kretschmer
University of Kansas

Marsha V. Krotseng
State College and University Systems of West Virginia

George D. Kuh
Indiana University–Bloomington

Daniel T. Layzell
University of Wisconsin System

Patrick G. Love
Kent State University

Cheryl D. Lovell
State Higher Education Executive Officers

Meredith Jane Ludwig
American Association of State Colleges and Universities

Dewayne Matthews
Western Interstate Commission for Higher Education

Mantha V. Mehallis
Florida Atlantic University

Toby Milton
Essex Community College

James R. Mingle
State Higher Education Executive Officers

John A. Muffo
Virginia Polytechnic Institute and State University

L. Jackson Newell
Deep Springs College

James C. Palmer
Illinois State University

Robert A. Rhoads
The Pennsylvania State University

G. Jeremiah Ryan
Harford Community College

Mary Ann Danowitz Sagaria
The Ohio State University

Daryl G. Smith
The Claremont Graduate School

William G. Tierney
University of Southern California

Susan B. Twombly
University of Kansas

Robert A. Walhaus
University of Illinois–Chicago

Harold Wechsler
University of Rochester

Elizabeth J. Whitt
University of Illinois–Chicago

Michael J. Worth
The George Washington University

RECENT TITLES

Volume 25 ASHE-ERIC Higher Education Reports

1. A Culture for Academic Excellence: Implementing the Quality Principles in Higher Education
   Jann E. Freed, Marie R. Klugman, and Jonathan D. Fife

2. From Discipline to Development: Rethinking Student Conduct in Higher Education
   Michael Dannells

Volume 24 ASHE-ERIC Higher Education Reports

1. Tenure, Promotion, and Reappointment: Legal and Administrative Implications (951)
   Benjamin Baez and John A. Centra

2. Taking Teaching Seriously: Meeting the Challenge of Instructional Improvement (952)
   Michael B. Paulsen and Kenneth A. Feldman

3. Empowering the Faculty: Mentoring Redirected and Renewed (953)
   Gaye Luna and Deborah L. Cullen

4. Enhancing Student Learning: Intellectual, Social, and Emotional Integration (954)
   Anne Goodsell Love and Patrick G. Love

5. Benchmarking in Higher Education: Adapting Best Practices to Improve Quality (955)
   Jeffrey W. Alstete

6. Models for Improving College Teaching: A Faculty Resource (956)
   Jon E. Travis

7. Experiential Learning in Higher Education: Linking Classroom and Community (957)
   Jeffrey A. Cantor

8. Successful Faculty Development and Evaluation: The Complete Teaching Portfolio (958)
   John P. Murray

Volume 23 ASHE-ERIC Higher Education Reports

1. The Advisory Committee Advantage: Creating an Effective Strategy for Programmatic Improvement (941)
   Lee Teitel

2. Collaborative Peer Review: The Role of Faculty in Improving College Teaching (942)
   Larry Keig and Michael D. Waggoner

3. Prices, Productivity, and Investment: Assessing Financial Strategies in Higher Education (943)
   Edward P. St. John

Volume 21 ASHE-ERIC Higher Education Reports

1. The Leadership Compass: Values and Ethics in Higher Education (921)
   John R. Wilcox and Susan L. Ebbs

2. Preparing for a Global Community: Achieving an International Perspective in Higher Education (922)
   Sarah M. Pickert

3. Quality: Transforming Postsecondary Education (923)
   Ellen Earle Chaffee and Lawrence A. Sherr

4. Faculty Job Satisfaction: Women and Minorities in Peril (924)
   Martha Wingard Tack and Carol Logan Patitu

5. Reconciling Rights and Responsibilities of Colleges and Students: Offensive Speech, Assembly, Drug Testing, and Safety (925)
   Annette Gibbs

6. Creating Distinctiveness: Lessons from Uncommon Colleges and Universities (926)
   Barbara K. Townsend, L. Jackson Newell, and Michael D. Wiese

7. Instituting Enduring Innovations: Achieving Continuity of Change in Higher Education (927)
   Barbara K. Curry

8. Crossing Pedagogical Oceans: International Teaching Assistants in U.S. Undergraduate Education (928)
   Rosslyn M. Smith, Patricia Byrd, Gayle L. Nelson, Ralph Pat Barrett, and Janet C. Constantinides

_____ Please begin my subscription to the current year's *ASHE-ERIC Higher Education Reports* (Volume 25) at $120.00, over 33% off the cover price, starting with Report 1. _____

_____ Please send a complete set of Volume ___ *ASHE-ERIC Higher Education Reports* at $120.00, over 33% off the cover price. _____

Individual reports are available for $24.00 and include the cost of shipping and handling.

SHIPPING POLICY:

- Books are sent UPS Ground or equivalent. For faster delivery, call for charges.
- Alaska, Hawaii, U.S. Territories, and Foreign Countries, please call for shipping information.
- Order will be shipped within 24 hours after receipt of request.
- Orders of 10 or more books, call for shipping information.

All prices shown are subject to change.

Returns: No cash refunds—credit will be applied to future orders.

PLEASE SEND ME THE FOLLOWING REPORTS:

Quantity	Volume/No.	Title	Amount

Please check one of the following:

☐ Check enclosed, payable to GWU-ERIC.
☐ Purchase order attached.
☐ Charge my credit card indicated below:
   ☐ Visa   ☐ MasterCard

Subtotal: _____
Less Discount: _____
Total Due: _____

Expiration Date_____

Name_____

Title_____

Institution _____

Address_____

City _____ State _____ Zip_____

Phone _____ Fax _____ Telex_____

Signature _____ Date_____

SEND ALL ORDERS TO: ASHE-ERIC Higher Education Reports
The George Washington University
One Dupont Cir., Ste. 630, Washington, DC 20036-1183
Phone: (202) 296-2597 • Toll-free: 800-773-ERIC
FAX: (202) 452-1844
http://www.gwu.edu/~eriche